The Next Best Place

Also by Julie Tate-Libby

The Good Way: A Himalayan Journey
Koehler Books, 2019

Praise for *The Next Best Place*

"This is a fun, informative book written by an anthropologist who turns her discerning lens on herself and the valley where she grew up. This is no dry, academic study, but an intimate, lively dive into a place that thrives."

    Diana Hottell, *The Whole Damn Valley* and *Earlier Times*

"Julie Tate-Libby has a rare talent for melding heart and head. In *The Next Best Place* she intertwines fiercely personal stories from her own life with small bites of academic research to illuminate the Methow Valley's seismic cultural and economic shifts. What does it mean when a quiet valley that's home to gritty characters working the land and freely roaming the hills evolves into an economically stratified place with newcomers focused on recreation? Tate-Libby takes us beyond the No Trespassing signs in this moving meditation on the meaning of social class and 'home.'"

    Karen West, *Bound for the Methow*

"Julie writes with clarity and first-hand experience, offering a vivid, heartfelt window into life in rural America. Her story is infused with grit, grace, and humor, capturing the rhythms of a place—of a people—often overlooked. Through her eyes, we witness the complex ripple effects of amenity migration, revealing how even well-intentioned choices can reshape communities in unexpected ways. This is more than a personal journey—it's an invitation to reflect on our own roles in the places we touch. You'll be glad you accepted it."

    Don Linnertz, TwispWorks Executive Director (Retired)

The Next Best Place

Love Letters to a Mountain Town in the American West

Julie Tate-Libby

Methow Press
Twisp, Washington 98856

© 2025 by Julie Tate-Libby

Published by Methow Press
P.O. Box 1213, Twisp, WA 98856
www.methowpress.com

Printed in the United States of America

All rights reserved. No part of this publication may be reproduced, stored in a retrieval system, or transmitted in any form or by any means—for example, electronic, photocopy, or recording—without the prior written permission of the publisher. The only exception is brief quotations in printed reviews.

ISBN: 979-8-9913567-7-0

Cover image by the Tate family. Used by permission.

Contents

Prologue i
The Dog Years 1
A Home of My Own 19
Housecleaning 31
Puckett Creek 45
Amenity Migration 55
Summer at the End of the World 71
The Farm 85
Moving to the Next Best Place 97
The Wild 111
Living with Fire 125
Study Group 141
The Red Coats 157
Mishaps 171
Belonging 187
The Hunger Games 199
The Good Life 213
Postscript 231
Acknowledgements 235

Prologue

Mountain towns throughout the American West have experienced a seismic shift over the past few decades. During the 1990s and 2000s ranching, farming, and resource-dependent industries gave way to tourism and recreation economies. Gritty local bars turned into coffee houses and breweries. Hardware stores started selling Martha Stewart Living outdoor furniture collections, and gas stations turned into organic food stores.

The Covid-19 pandemic did not change this trajectory, but it did amplify it. Between 2020 and 2022, communities in Colorado, Wyoming, Montana, Oregon, and Washington experienced record growth and doubling property prices as remote workers and second homeowners flocked to rural communities. A recent study by the Northwest Colorado Council of Governments found that second homeowners and remote workers in five different regions spent significantly more time in these communities during the pandemic and planned to do so in the future. Industry forecasts suggest that by the end of this year, 22% of all employees will work remotely; further, 73% of all workers prefer a hybrid option. The changes in rural communities across the West are here to stay, and the glimpses we have of a pre-recreational past are swiftly receding into anecdote and memory.

I have been writing this book in my head for the last thirty years. While I waited tables, served coffee, and cleaned houses, a voice in my mind kept narrating events, tucking away particular stories for later. After moving back from New Zealand, where I received my PhD in amenity migration, I had visions of applying my dissertation framework to the Methow Valley, my own mountain town in Washington State. I wanted to dazzle people with a brilliantly crafted critique of class, place, and otherness. I started drafts and deleted them. I wrote other things. I kept coming back to the idea, but I couldn't figure out which voice to use. I wanted to highlight specific themes, but I also wanted to tell a story.

One afternoon during the Covid-19 pandemic, I sat down to begin, and these chapters wrote themselves.

Many books about place are written from an outside perspective, which can be illuminating and sometimes more honest and objective than a local one. Mine is not such a perspective. I grew up in the Methow Valley, and my stories are embedded in the years I spent attending school, owning two small businesses, raising daughters, and trying to carve out a life of my own here. But in many ways, I am also an outsider. I left and returned over the years—to Asia, Africa, the Pacific Islands, and elsewhere. I received a master's degree and a PhD in anthropology and have spent most of my life studying people in other places. All the while, I have studied myself within this community. I may yet write the academic version of this book, but this is not it. The stories that follow are personal. They're stories about my life in this place, surrounded by people I know and love.

Although I critique how I see the valley changing, I am part of the change. I own a beautiful home in the Methow Valley, one I could not afford to buy today. I appreciate organic food and good wine. Many of my friends moved here in the last few years with remote jobs and fat paychecks. I don't necessarily fit in with the old-timers or locals anymore, but I want their voices to be heard. The valley that they homesteaded and loved is changing. Wine bars, a movie theater, multi-million-dollar homes designed by famous architects are all part of a shifting landscape. I want people to feel what the character of this place was prior to their arrival.

I don't know if other waitresses write books, but I have always loved ethnographies that highlight members of the working class. They remind me of where I came from. I am no longer a waitress, but this book is for people who traverse class boundaries. Having run back and forth across those boundaries my entire life, I feel I can speak to multiple sides.

This book is also for anyone who loved or loves a mountain town in the American West. It's for anyone who has just moved to or is considering moving to a mountain town. While the stories take place in a particular valley, one which is four hours from Seattle, they could have taken place anywhere.

Finally, this book is for those who live in the Methow Valley, and for those who are coming.

Consider this my love letter to the mountain town I once knew. And if you're new to such a town, please tread softly.

Julie Tate-Libby
Twisp, Washington
June 1, 2025

The Dog Years

Someone once told me that each year working in Winthrop took seven off your life—like calculating a dog's age. Seven to one.

The dog years. I think about this now, because I started waiting tables in Winthrop when I was thirteen.

My first job was at a tiny Italian café called Giovanni's. They served pizza, salads, bakery goods, and espresso—which back then was a novelty. Two months later, the manager from a resort down the road offered me another job, so by the time school got out for the summer, I was working about sixteen hours a day. Every morning, Dad dropped me off for work at the café at 7 AM. Bleary and nervous, I'd make espresso, take orders, and serve baked goods until mid-afternoon. At 2:30, in a sweltering one hundred degrees, I'd trudge a mile down the highway to my next job bussing tables at the Virginian Resort.

Food service is an industry like no other. It's not an emergency room. There are no coronary triple bypasses, no surgeries, no dramatic life and death situations—but if you stepped into a restaurant kitchen at the height of a slam, an emergency room would be the closest thing to it.

The guy washing dishes hurls plates and glasses into an overflowing machine. Line cooks are buried three to four deep along a flaming, sizzling row of fryers, grills, and burners. Waitresses scream last-minute orders, and the chef hurls curses at everyone.

The Virginian was a particularly colorful workplace. Once, in the middle of a slam, one of the line cooks lost his temper over a returned plate.

"It's what?" He leaned over the warming bar, sweat trickling down his lined face.

"They said it's not done!" The waitress shoved the plate toward him.

He dug his finger into the offending steak. "Medium fucking rare, that's what it is. Maybe they should go back to fucking eating school."

Unloading a tray of dirty dishes, I ducked as the plate sailed over my head. In a miraculous stroke of timing, the kitchen doors swung open at that exact moment, and the steak hurtled into the dining room. The customers, horrified to see their filet mignon flying towards their table, left in an uproar, threatening to sue. I would like to be able to say that this was an anomaly at the Virginian, but over the course of the six years I worked there, I saw many things thrown across the kitchen. Salad, dinner rolls, plates, and even knives.

Giovanni's was tame compared to the Virginian. It was smaller, and the food was prepared in a microwave oven, which meant there were no line cooks and kitchen staff—just me and the owner, a hardcore Republican and longtime restaurateur from Tonasket. He taught me the first cardinal rule of any restaurant: "If you've got time to lean, you've got time to clean," he'd yell as I headed out with a tray full of water glasses.

I was already a conscientious worker and would have died if caught "leaning," whatever that meant, but for this man I positively ran. When I wasn't trying out my social skills on customers, I Windexed the bakery case and the windows. I wiped down the tables with bleach water and scrubbed the espresso machine with a toothbrush. I even cleaned the salt and pepper shakers with a toothpick. Who knew that condiment holders could get so greasy?

The hardest part was greeting a new table. At thirteen, my voice was soft and high-pitched. No one could hear me. I'd muster all the gumption I could to call out a hearty, "Hi there, how are you today?"

"What's that?" an old man would ask.

"How are you today?" I'd repeat loudly.

Waiting tables is not for the faint of heart. You have to adopt a certain personality—insanely cheerful, full of energy, and infinitely knowledgeable. You must know, immediately, everything that you're out of *before* you're out of it. You must know the ingredients in every dish—which back in those days came in an assortment of cans from Food Services of America.

"What's in your biscuits and gravy?" a plump woman in her sixties once asked.

"Oh, you know, sausage and gravy." I had no idea. I was a vegetarian.

"Hmm." The woman glanced at the menu. "Is it homemade?"

The dreaded question. The one thing I did know, of course, was that *nothing* was homemade. I paused.

"No," I said, a smile pasted firm. "It actually comes from a can. But people love it."

The woman leaned back in her chair and studied me. "I don't believe you."

"Huh?" I didn't know what to say.

"You have shifty eyes."

I blinked. What was wrong with my eyes?

"I'll get the biscuits and gravy."

Later, when I took her empty plate, she glared. "That was homemade. I can always tell."

Rule number two in a restaurant: Tell customers only what they want to hear. People don't want to know that their food came from a can. They would rather believe that someone spent the better part of the night preparing it, even in a restaurant that doesn't have a kitchen.

Personality is also important. If you're not confident, people get uncomfortable. For me, this was a big problem.

"Just chat with them," the owner told me, shooing me out to make small talk while he watched from the window. I hated this. It was bad enough that I had acne and was so shy I sent my sister to the counter to ask for ketchup packets at McDonald's, but having your boss watch you founder in conversation was too much.

There's something interesting about having to make small talk with strangers. The anthropologist Bronislaw Malinowski first coined the term "phatic communication" to describe the purposeless but highly ritualized linguistic banter he observed among Pacific Islanders.

Malinowski said that meaningless conversation wasn't about communicating information, but rather about establishing bonds of sociality between participants. In other words, small talk.

Waiting tables requires a meticulous kind of small talk, in which the server carries the conversation for the customers, putting them at ease and making them feel welcome. It establishes a fictitious bond between customers and server, one in which the server plays a subservient role for the procurement of a tip. The relationship begins when customers enter the premises and ends the minute they leave. During this time, everything a customer says is funny and witty. There are no stupid questions, and the customer is infinitely wise and knowledgeable. Not only does small talk establish these roles, it quickly progresses to intimate, non-verbal communication. For the hour it takes to dine at the establishment, the server can read the customers' thoughts and desires like a long-suffering wife.

A customer sighs and pushes away the plates.

The server scoops it up. "Anything else I can get you?"

"No, that'll be all."

The server nods and returns with the bill, which they discreetly hand to the correct person. No words are exchanged, only a glance between the server and customer. The transaction is almost complete.

Waiting tables in Winthrop added the component of playing "the local" to tourists from Seattle and the west side of the Cascade mountains.

"They got a school around here, or does everyone homeschool?"

"No, we have a school."

"You go there?"

"Yes."

"Bet it's pretty small. Is it a good school?"

I never knew how to answer this question. Were they asking if I, personally, liked it or if it was statistically considered a "good" school? At thirteen I didn't know the answer to either question. School was something you did. It didn't matter whether you liked it or not. Implicit in these interactions was the understanding that Seattle schools were better than Liberty Bell, which made Methow kids inferior to Seattle kids. The interaction worked to reinforce the general stereotype and allow customers to leave feeling like they were not only exemplary in their choice of vacation, but in their choice of residence.

Sometimes tourist families plied me for insider information.

"So, where's the best place to go swimming around here?"

"Pearrygin Lake is nice." Pearrygin Lake had leeches, swimmer's itch, and four hundred campsites full of screaming children and dogs. No one swam there except tourists.

"Yeah, we went there yesterday. I mean, where do the locals go?"

Now I faced a dilemma. I could tell them where people actually swam and risk the chance of running into them tomorrow, or I could lie and keep them congregated with everyone else.

"Well, Patterson is also nice."

"Is that where you go?"

"Sometimes."

"How do you get there?"

I didn't mind playing the knowledgeable host. Nor did I mind pretending to be inferior to their kids. I had big plans, and their tip was going help me make them happen.

With my boss watching from the window, I walked out to the nearest table.

"How's your house Merlot?"

"Excellent."

"Is it very sweet? Because I don't like sweet."

Being thirteen and having never tasted wine, I answered wisely. "It has just an edge to it."

◆◆◆◆

Working in restaurants taught me to multi-task and think quickly. It taught me to lie when necessary. It taught me to push through a long day and put in an extra four hours when I didn't think I could.

Eventually, the little Italian café burned down and resurfaced several years later across the street with a new name, the Grubstake & Co. By then, I was finished with college, recently married, but still wondering what to do with my life. Kenny and I had moved home for the summer while I applied for graduate programs, and once again I found myself working double shifts at the restaurant.

It was a busy summer. Tourists flocked to Winthrop in droves. July's sales were up by thirty percent, and August was looking to be even busier. One weekend, the cook went on a bender and disappeared. The owners approached me the following day.

"Julie, we'd like to have a talk with you and your husband."

Kenny? Why did they want to talk to Kenny? He worked down the road as a landscaper planting trees. We both made minimum wage, $7.25 an hour. Kenny had never worked in a restaurant before, and the only thing he knew about cafés was how much money he liked to spend at them. Double tall Americanos, brownies, ham and cheese croissants, and slices of pizza.

But the owners insisted, going so far as to invite us to their house for dinner. They lived several miles up Lost River in an enormous, hand-crafted waterfront log home. I was instantly enamored with the flowers, rock walls, and stand of aspens outside. The house had hand-tiled floors and enormous windows that looked into the surrounding woodlands. I knew nothing about houses or property values, but even I, at twenty-two years old, could smell money.

They poured us wine and set out a cheese plate. We laughed and talked late into the night. By the time we left, we had agreed on sale terms for the restaurant. I didn't want to buy the Grubstake, but I did want the life they showed us. I was ready for anything.

Kenny and I took over the Grubstake on August 1, 1999. It remains to this day one of the busiest summers on record. We worked seventeen to eighteen hours a day, sometimes crashing in our car for a few hours of sleep before we had to do it all over again. We learned to bake bread and pizza dough. We learned how to poach an egg and make an omelet. We learned how to place orders on Sundays and Wednesdays, how to cross-reference a menu to avoid food waste, and how to keep track of daily sales and receipts.

Kenny managed the outside coffee bar and dining room, while I took over the kitchen. The kitchen was my tiny world. If I stretched out my hands in either direction, I could literally touch the pizza ovens, the makeup counter, the kitchen sink, and the serving bar at the same time. We cooked breakfast over a four-burner propane camp stove, which we disassembled at lunchtime to make room for pizza and salad.

You wouldn't believe the amount of food we managed to serve out of that kitchen. One of the first mornings after we took over the restaurant, we did eighty-eight breakfasts in three hours. The tickets kept appearing along the magnetic strip over the makeup counter. Kenny dashed in and out of the kitchen, his white apron flapping.

"*Order up, order up!*" he screamed, as his glasses slipped down his nose.

I didn't have time to answer. The waitresses had long since quit trying to clear their plates. They simply heaved the trays into the sink and ran out again. Faintly, over the din of the ovens and the swamp cooler, I could hear the dull roar of a crowded dining room. I had only made five omelets in my life. I had no idea if we had prepped enough to get through the slam. I hadn't even memorized the menu yet. Where was the bread? How many cases of eggs had we ordered?

Just as I started to panic, something happened that would occur frequently over the next few years. The noise and chaos faded. I could hear the beating of my heart, quietly at first, then deep and steady. I breathed in. I breathed out. The panic faded. My hands moved of their own accord. Crack eggs, beat. Add milk. Roasted garlic, sundried tomatoes, mushrooms—sauté. Toast down. Butter. Garnish. Order up! It became a dance. A slow-motion box-step with my hands moving every second. The plates were warm. The orders sailed out of the kitchen with clockwork precision. I was in the flow.

When I finally plated the last order and glanced at the clock, I couldn't believe it was already 11 AM. Lunchtime. We had made it through the busiest breakfast in the Grubstake's history.

That first summer passed in a blur of early mornings and late nights, fueled by a million double-short Americanos. My main memories of that time are of the slant of the sun on the outdoor deck as summer receded into fall and then into winter. The light was always changing—from early morning clear and translucent, to lazy afternoons, golden and hot.

There were also the customers. We got to know them by their coffee drinks. There was double-dry cappuccino Ron and his wife double-extra hot-latte Kathy. There was also double-light-on-the-chocolate mocha Ron and his wife whose drink, and therefore whose name, I never remembered. There was double-Americano extra-cream-with-honey Paul and triple-short-whole-milk latte Betsy.

These people and many others drifted into our lives nearly every day. They grew accustomed to us serving them. If one of the employees was on the coffee bar, they'd say, "Oh, I'll wait for Kenny. He knows what I get."

It was somewhat flattering that they only wanted my cooking and Kenny's coffee, but it was also exhausting. Would we ever be able to leave again? Years later, when our daughter Annika was born, people warned me that having kids was a 24-7 ordeal. I knew what this was like. The Grubstake was our child. An ill-tempered, hungry child that demanded constant attention and offered little forgiveness, especially for minor transgressions.

One afternoon in October, an elderly gentleman and his wife were leaving the restaurant when she tripped on the boardwalk and fell. She landed on her side and twisted her ankle. I was pretty sure she was okay, because once we hauled her up, she walked just fine. Her husband, however, demanded to see a copy of our insurance policy. Insurance policy? Did we have one? My mind raced. Vaguely, I remembered signing something official with the insurance agent after we bought the café. Was this what they were talking about? At twenty-two, neither Kenny nor I had insurance, health or otherwise. We crossed our fingers and hoped we wouldn't get sick. Health insurance was one of those Big Adult things I'd put off for the future.

"Okay, sure. Do you want some ice?" I hurried off to find the policy, my heart racing.

When I returned, the woman was sitting on a bench, clutching her foot. "We're going to need to speak to your lawyer," the husband announced.

Lawyer? We didn't have a lawyer. Was he kidding? We didn't have a banker or a doctor. We didn't even own a house. We lived out of our car. My heart raced. My throat went dry. This was it. They were going to sue us and take the $8,000 I had saved up for a house. Suddenly I hated the couple. Him, with his tweedy coat and pince-nez glasses. I hated her for being old and falling on the sidewalk.

It wasn't even *our* sidewalk—it was the town boardwalk in Winthrop, which had a thousand uneven planks. It was supposed to look "Old West."

I crouched next to the woman, pressing ice to her ankle, inwardly cursing. Outwardly, I smiled and tried to make small talk.

"Yeah, that boardwalk. You know I think they built it back in the '70s or something."

The man grumbled into his handkerchief and blew his nose.

"Your ankle's starting to look better. Do you want to try to walk to your car?"

At last I got the lady into her car. The man glared at me over his glasses. "We'll be in touch with your insurance company." He slammed the car door and sped away.

I turned back to my kitchen, shaking. *Everything*. We were going to lose everything.

I didn't realize then that, had the couple actually filed a claim, the insurance company would have paid it—not us. As it turned out, we never heard from the couple again, but I'll never forget the feeling of complete and utter panic. We were so young. It felt like the world had us by the throat.

◆◆◆◆

Over the next few years, business continued to increase. We ditched the canned items for homemade recipes and started ordering seasonal organic produce. We planted sunflowers along the outside deck and remodeled the dining room. But my biggest pet peeve remained—the outdoor sluice box. The previous owners had named the place the Grubstake after an

Old West mining term. A grubstake was a temporary line of credit for goods at a store before the miner went out for the season: The company "staked" the miner with equipment and makings for grub... a grub-stake. When he returned, he repaid the grubstake with his earnings in gold. In fitting with this theme, the couple had constructed a giant wooden sluice box that ran from the upper deck to the lower, with water running through it. Kids could pan for gold while their parents ate lunch.

Not only did I abhor the Western theme, I detested the kids who flocked to the water feature. I didn't have children, and to my twenty-two-year-old sensibilities, the sluice box was embarrassing. It was tacky.

But it did bring business. In retrospect, I can see how nice it would be to lunch peacefully while your kids splashed in a box of water, but by the time I was old enough to appreciate the appeal, we had moved on from the Grubstake and the chaotic five years we spent there.

It's terrible to say you hate kids. No one does so publicly, but after hundreds of afternoons catering to mothers with herds of kids, I really came to that point.

The kids would arrive first, screaming with joy before tripping on the deck. Their delight quickly turned to howls of rage over a skinned knee or a hornet sting. August was a particularly loathsome month for hornets and children. By the end of the summer, as the wasps started to congregate in their love for both food and water, their mothers' patience wore as thin as my own.

"Excuse me! Do you have a bee sting kit? You know those little capsules of green stuff?" The mothers were frantic, irritated at another meltdown and counting the days until school started in September.

"We have baking soda." I'd smile brightly and hand over paper towels and a ramekin of water and baking soda.

"You mean you really don't carry bee sting kits? Unbelievable!" I'd hear the mother say to her friend. "They should at least carry kits."

Meanwhile the kid was thrashing about on the deck, going berserk while another hornet buzzed around his head. The family dog would join the fun, lunging for the sluice box, upsetting the stroller, and grabbing a slice of pizza in the process.

Since I was the cook, I got to watch these proceedings, sometimes with great interest, through a tiny window in the door of my kitchen that faced the deck. With the glare of the sun on the glass, no one could see in, but I could see out.

I watched hundreds of families through that window. I watched fathers sigh and roll their eyes, the mothers tight-lipped and irritated. I watched the kids run around, oblivious to the chaos they created. I suppose some families were happy and enjoyed each other's company, but what impressed itself upon me was the stress that emanated from families on vacation trying to have fun… and failing.

Years later, as a young mother myself in New Zealand with two toddlers and an irritable husband, I would remember those families with a pang of regret. I should have been kinder. They were doing the best they could.

Labor Day was always the worst—and the best—weekend. The worst, because it was one of the busiest, and by then we were completely burned out—and the best because it had an end. School would start on Tuesday, and everybody had to go home. By Monday afternoon, I'd watch from my window as the last of the tourist cars turned left at the four-way stop, heading back to Seattle. It was a lovely feeling.

One Monday afternoon after a Labor Day weekend, I was sitting on the flour bin in the kitchen, enjoying an iced Americano when I saw a red Chevrolet van pull up to the coffee bar.

"No…" I muttered as I watched six kids hang their heads out the windows. Fingerprints littered the windshield. A dog barked from inside. A toddler screamed. A maternally heavy, pale woman with frizzy hair emerged from the van. She glanced around as if looking for a bathroom.

No public restroom. Sorry. I sucked down my iced Americano.

She walked up to the coffee bar. No one was there. She strode up to my window and peered inside. I felt a perverse desire to hide from her, so instead of walking out to the coffee bar to greet her, I did nothing. She didn't see me, but she did spy the overflowing garbage can by the door. Triumphantly, she hurried back to the van and emerged with several McDonald's Happy Meal boxes, thirty-two-ounce Slurpee cups, and a plastic bag full of dirty diapers.

"No!" I whispered from my perch in the kitchen. She *wouldn't*.

She did.

Glancing around once more, the woman shoved her garbage into the overflowing can. The diapers landed on the deck. Coffee cups spilled over. The woman glared at the can and kicked it, then shrugged and turned to go.

I watched in horror as she walked back towards her van. Her white legs trudged determinedly. The woman was moving so quickly she didn't see one of the hanging flower baskets that hung from the coffee bar. When her forehead struck, the impact knocked her backwards. She lay on her back for a moment, stunned. I stared, not daring to move. After a second, she shook herself and staggered to her feet. Glancing around a last time, she hurried to the van and slammed the door. The red Chevrolet peeled out, dogs and kids screaming from the open windows.

Inside the kitchen, I collapsed on the flour bin, laughing. I couldn't help it. I laughed and laughed. I laughed so hard that tears ran down my face. I laughed until I cried, and still I laughed. It seemed to epitomize the whole summer. The heat, the kids, the tourists, the wasps. Every time I remembered the image of her falling backwards, I laughed again.

Psychologists say that laughing and crying are coping mechanisms for when your emotions get overloaded. They also say that laughing at someone else's pain is a substitute for empathy and we laugh because we fear feeling the full extent of their emotions. Maybe I laughed because for most of my life I had to be courteous to people like that woman. For years, rude strangers had ruled my waking hours. When they behaved badly, I'd had to behave perfectly.

I would like to think that humans are mostly good. Today, I do. But during the years working in Winthrop, I struggled with humanity. I really did. And you know what? I still laugh at the memory of the woman hitting her head.

I tell this story and others to my daughters. They've become treasured family anecdotes. And in the telling, the memories, many of which were not funny at the time, have changed.

Through the alchemy of time and distance, my years as a waitress have been transformed. Where I was once young and insecure, hoping to earn my way into a middle-class life, I am now the age of those mothers—and I have indeed made my way into a middle-class life. Where I felt helpless before, I feel kinder today.

I look back at those years with a certain fondness. Would I repeat them? Never. But I'm grateful for the dog years. Every one of them.

A Home of My Own

I was twelve years old when my family moved to the Methow Valley. After days of house hunting with a real estate agent, I still remember the moment we found our home.

As we followed the agent's car down the long dirt driveway, we drove past a barn with horses and acres of green alfalfa. At the end of the driveway, a white picket fence surrounded an old farmhouse. Craggy Chinese elms and a stand of quaking aspen shaded the yard. Orange day lilies bloomed along the porch. A dog barked. Beyond the house ran the river. Rolling down the window, I glimpsed water sparkling through the trees. Bits of cotton blew in the breeze. I took a deep breath—pine trees, river, the scent of alfalfa blooms. I felt like Anne of Green Gables. There was the barn, the green fields, the river, a forest, and flower beds everywhere. I was home.

I've always loved homes. It's not the house or the architectural style. It's that intangible feeling that pervades a place. It's the view from the porch or the way the house nestles in the landscape. The trees in the yard. Some places make you feel like you belong. When we moved to the farm in 1989, I felt like I had been waiting my entire life to find home. Given that I was only twelve, "my entire life" wasn't much time, but I grieved the years I'd spent without the farm.

One day, I found an old newspaper from 1923 stapled inside the walls for insulation. I spent the next few months hunting for historic treasures. I dug up farming equipment, tools, anything that looked old. I set up a museum in the basement with the artifacts I'd collected. A sewing machine. An iron. An old leather boot.

Eventually I found the original property map and traced the whole parcel—160 acres of homestead, whittled down to just thirty. Someday, I vowed, I'd buy the property around our house and reunite the farm.

I made my first offer on a house at the age of twenty. While other kids were hanging out with friends and going to parties, I was busy waiting tables and saving tip money. It wasn't the riverfront property around our farm but the house I rented one summer during college. Every night, I'd empty my tip jar and count the money. There was something satisfying about touching that money, organizing it into piles, and adding it again and again. I had saved $8,000. In 1997, that was enough for a down payment on a house.

The house, built in the 1930s, had once been an apple picker's cabin. Other than the rattlesnakes that lived under the front porch, I loved that house. It had hardwood floors and a kitchen that overlooked the river. At night, a cool breeze from the ridge blew through the windows.

My Dad helped me write the offer. The property included twenty acres of dry hillside and a well that yielded 8.6 gallons a minute, which wasn't bad. The owners were asking $92,000 for the place. I offered $88,000. After three days of anxious waiting, I got the news. They had rejected my offer. I was devastated but no less determined to have a place of my own one day.

Two years later, I found myself closer to homeownership. Now that I was married and with a college degree under my belt, my husband, Kenny, and I made an offer on a newly built 730-square-foot cabin. Like my first house, it had wood floors and big windows. I was still waiting tables—albeit in my own restaurant where Kenny and I worked eighteen hours a day. We didn't need a house, as much as a landing pad to crash on. We'd been sleeping in our car and camping for six months to save money. This time, we had $13,000 down on a $108,000 house. We bought the house and flipped it a year later, making $30,000 in the process and paying off our loan with the tip money and cash we managed to siphon through the restaurant. This was our beginning of homeownership in the Methow.

The second home we bought turned out to be one of the great loves of my life. But it was a rough start. The night we moved in, the smell of mice and dry rot drove us outside, where we ended up sleeping on the back deck, which was not yet a deck, but a platform covered in tar with a twenty-foot drop-off. In the morning, our bags had melted into the tar. We didn't care. The sky was clear and blue. Water gurgled from the creek below. Ravens called back and forth in the pine trees. It was perfectly still. I knew I was home.

The house was an almost condemnable log cabin on twenty acres of ponderosa pine forest. You couldn't actually see the house because it was hidden by a hedge of broken-down cars, tires, wheel beds, and even a train engine. The most defining characteristic of the place was a 1970s yellow school bus that had apparently died in the front yard. People referred to the property as "the one with the bus and all the dogs."

When my mother-in-law first saw it, she burst into tears. I thought it was a mistake to show Kenny's parents the house before it closed, but he insisted. When Jan stepped from the car in her matching quilted purse and coat, the owners were having a campfire in the driveway. They'd been clearing junk off the property for two months. They were almost done—but the bus was still there.

Jan stepped over a beer can. "Is that a school bus?" She turned to Kenny.

One of the men spoke up. "Yep, sure is. Don't think I ever seen that bus move. You seen it move, Charlie?" He spat a stream of brown tobacco juice into the fire.

Charlie pulled the tab on another beer. "Nope. Hell, I remember when Gary parked that thing up here. Never did run."

A kid with a baseball cap piped up. "Remember when it used to be a chicken coop?"

Charlie took a swig of beer. "Yep, first it was a chicken coop, then it was a meat locker, then... Hell, I think we used it for a shit house."

That's when my mother-in-law burst into tears.

"I don't know why you would want to live that way," she told me later, wiping mascara from her eyes. "I just can't imagine."

But *we* could.

We lived in a wall tent for the summer. Six months pregnant with our first daughter, Annika, I made the forty-mile trip to town every day and worked the restaurant, while Kenny and his best friend tore apart the house. They had never built a house or remodeled one. They had never worked with logs. They didn't have any tools. At twenty-five years old, they had ponytails, Neil Young, and Crosby, Stills & Nash. Beer and pizza from the restaurant helped as well.

At night I'd come home from the restaurant bearing food. Often, music still blared. Bats flitted in the porch lights. Saws whined. We cleared a patch of sawdust off the new front porch and ate dinner at ten or eleven at night.

We worked all summer, cutting away dry rot, jacking up the house, and putting on a new roof, new metal, and new floors. I rarely ventured upstairs. It scared me a little. One afternoon, I took a deep breath and climbed the rickety steps to the second floor. Plastic sheets stapled to the windows flapped in the breeze. Apparently, five Dobermans had lived in the house, and the exposed subfloor reeked of urine. The upstairs bathroom had a hole near the toilet where you could see into the downstairs bathroom, which gave me a sense of vertigo and a creepy, voyeuristic feeling.

Peering outside through a hole in the plastic, I stood where one day the primary bedroom would be. From here I could see down onto the creek bank. A steep, green ridge ran up the opposite side covered with old-growth ponderosa pines. Far below, water glinted through the elderberry and vine maple.

I went to school with the kids who had grown up in this house. One of the girls had dropped out in the eighth grade. The boys worked in logging and left the valley, one by one. Standing there in the upstairs of their childhood home, I imagined their life. Cigarette butts on the floor. Beer cans. Living in the middle of nowhere. Never doing school sports because their parents couldn't drive that far. Never having enough money to fix up the place. Now, touching the plastic where glass should have been, I remembered the siblings' shabby clothes and how kids on the bus made fun of them. I had grown up just six miles away, but it may as well have been another country.

The Methow is riddled with poverty, but it's hidden. Some of it goes back to the homesteader families, like my former husband's family—the Libbys. Ken is a Libby of Libby Creek, the creek on which I now stood, looking out the window. His great-great-grandfather A.C. Libby homesteaded in 1886.

A renowned drinker, horse trader, and jack-of-all-trades, A.C. built a cabin at the mouth of the creek and named it after himself. He married a woman named Sarah and had four boys, one of whom would become a traveling minister and my husband's great-grandfather. Another would go to World War II and return an alcoholic and drifter.

For a time, the Libbys were renowned in the valley. Like other homesteader families, some of whom remain today, their notoriety was based on stories of the backcountry, mining claims, ranching, fast cars, and drinking. Eventually, the Libby homestead burned down, and the family resettled up Twisp River. By the time my husband, Ken, moved to the Methow from Minnesota in search of his roots, the Libbys had all but disappeared. Only the name remained—Libby Creek and Libby Lake.

Homesteader families exist today, but they're hidden in the community. They don't fit in with the Microsoft retirees in Mazama or the young hippie kids on their organic farms. They won't be seen wearing Lycra ski gear or having a latte at the Mazama Store. Only if you knew their faces, which you might see at the Branding Iron in Twisp or at Hank's Deli, would you know that any old-timers had survived.

Today, the prominent people in the Methow are second homeowners and donors to the numerous non-profits. They're the new family from California whose kids ski Nordic and win most of the races. They're the new faces on every board and committee. They move in savvy circles. They have degrees from good schools. They show up for school and community events, to all the meetings and all the strategic planning sessions. Even the town mayors and police chiefs and the directors of nonprofits, almost anyone who's anyone, moved to the Methow within the last five or ten years.

◆◆◆◆

One summer afternoon, a few years after we moved up Libby Creek, a rancher and his son stopped by in search of their cows. I knew the man. His family had homesteaded with the Libbys and he loved to reminisce about the old days with anyone who would listen. Reluctantly, I found myself a captive audience. He and his son climbed out of the pickup truck.

"Howdy there, ma'am. Seen any cows lately?" The son tipped his hat.

"Yes, actually I saw a couple of them yesterday." I didn't mention that we'd run them up the creek on our bicycles.

"Yep." The rancher spit a long stream of tobacco juice. "Figured."

Silence.

"You're the Libby wife, aren't you?"

"Yes." I also didn't mention that I'd known the rancher since those early days at the farm. He owned the property upon which I routinely trespassed as a teenager. He didn't remember me.

"Yep, those Libbys… Quite a family. You know we knew them back then, right?"

"Yes, I remember." I glanced around, hoping for a diversion.

"My momma was a schoolteacher. She always talked about those Libby boys. Said they came to school without shoes. Sometimes no lunch. They had it kinda rough, you know."

"Yes, I've heard."

"One time, I 'member her saying it was winter. Cold out, lotsa snow. One of those boys came to school all beat up, and my momma—she said that was it. She took those boys home, and they stayed with us for a good while. My ma was always taking in kids."

"That was nice of her."

"Yeah. Those Libbys. You knew Cliff?"

Cliff was the son who went to World War II. I'd heard numerous stories about him, but he died long before I met Kenny.

"No, I never met him."

"Yep, that Cliff. He was a wild man. You know he useta ride his horse from Twisp River, clear up to Winthrop and have a drink at the bar. Then he'd ride on back at three or four in the morning. Best mountain man I ever met."

I nodded. It was hot. I wondered if the girls were waking up from their naps. Chickens clucked in the coop by the woodshed. I glanced towards the driveway. "Well, if I see any cows..."

"You know something?" The rancher shoved his hands into his pockets. "Seems like anymore, all these people moving here—they just want my land."

I blinked at the sudden turn in conversation. "Is that so?"

"Yeah. Everyone wants my land, but you know what?" He shook his head and gave me a wink as he turned to go.

"No one wants me. Nope, no one wants an old codger like me."

They drove off, waving cheerfully, but his words stuck. *No one wants me.*

It was true. No one wanted the old-timers anymore. Their time in the Methow had come and gone. Even when I moved here as a girl, they still had a certain clout. People talked about the Thurlows, the Libbys, the Christensens.

I thought about this as I walked inside. Sure, there were a lot of issues we differed on. Gun rights. The reintroduction of grizzlies and wolves. They were white, male, and patriarchs—but also hard workers, the type of people who never shirked from responsibility, whether it was pulling your daughter's car out of a snowbank or helping you change a flat tire up by Black Pine Lake.

But something else bothered me about his comment. The community they remembered, whether it was slightly mythologized or not, was different than the Methow today. The Methow had become—tame. Gentrified.

The backcountry was now a tourist destination. Roads were named after obscure philosophers or beat poets, not after the people who settled there. I remembered when we used to have one pair of skis that we took everywhere, wearing jeans.

Now the school had a Nordic ski team that trained kids for the Olympics.

As I cooked dinner that night, I couldn't shake the uncomfortable sense that I was more like the old-timers than not. If no one wanted *him* in the valley, where did that put me?

◆◆◆◆

By late fall, we moved into the downstairs of the house. Now almost nine months pregnant, I lay in front of the woodstove and reveled in the warmth. Winter was close, and we had done it. We had transformed a falling-down log cabin into a funky but beautiful home.

It took another seven years to finish the house and put in a yard, a garden, a shop, a deer fence. But I never regretted, not for one minute, the money or time we poured into that place. I loved Libby Creek like I loved my daughters. Sometimes, alone with them in the afternoons, as I made my rounds from the garden with its raised beds and perennials to the chicken coop with the dog at my side, I felt like the queen of a tiny kingdom.

It was as much home as the farm my family had moved to in 1989. That year my parents paid $135,000 for thirty acres of riverfront. A few summers ago, the same farm sold for $780,000 to a young couple from Seattle. I met them once at the Old Schoolhouse Brewery in Winthrop. They looked like kids.

By 2022 the median price of a home in the Methow Valley jumped to $478,000, and there's not much to choose from. As I write this, there are twenty-six homes on the market, only three under $500,000. Affordable housing has become a crisis. Coupled with the coronavirus pandemic, people are moving to the Methow *en masse*. For a valley with slightly more than 6,000 full-time residents, it feels a bit like a siege.

I wouldn't be able to afford a home today. Even with great credit and all the jobs I can finagle, a house in the Methow would be beyond my reach. I know we're lucky we got in when we did, but it makes me sad that economics are changing the valley forever. Along with the backcountry and families like the Libbys and my old-timer friend, we're losing a sense of place. I've always been grateful to own a home in the Methow, but tip money and fourteen-hour shifts won't get you there today.

I grew up with my Swedish relatives, who told me that anything was possible in the United States of America, and many of my Wenatchee Valley College students who moved from Mexico believe that. I'm not sure this is still possible.

Maybe somewhere else, but not in the Methow.

Housecleaning

One of my summer jobs during high school was cleaning houses.

I liked cleaning, especially nightly rentals. They had less stuff and I didn't have to deal with the homeowner. Back then, though, most of the rentals weren't so nice. Broken cupboard doors hung in the kitchens. Holes gaped in the screens. The vacuum rarely worked. Often, I found mouse droppings on the countertops. Sometimes, guests would run into me on their way out and complain about the house. I'd listen and nod sympathetically, but there was nothing I could do. I was just the cleaner. My pay scale varied throughout the years. Usually, I received an envelope with a $20 bill inside.

That was then. A few years ago, I heard that housecleaners were charging $35-$40 an hour—more than I was making teaching at the college. I was newly remarried and had moved to a farm outside of Twisp. *Maybe I should take up cleaning again*, I thought. The extra cash would be nice, and I could bring my teenage daughters, Annika and Mia. They would learn important skills like how to miter the corners while making a bed or how to clean an oven. Maybe they would enjoy cleaning and start picking up their rooms.

The girls were less enthusiastic about the prospect, but I told them I was saving money for our trip to Europe. They felt guilty.

Also, I bribed them with lunch at the Mazama Store.

The first afternoon I brought them along to clean was hot. The house sat nestled at the edge of a forest, overlooking green fields and the river. Its cottage-paned windows and wood floors reminded me of the house I grew up in. It was cool, well-insulated. Quiet.

The Saltillo tiled kitchen was outfitted with matching Fiestaware, and each drawer had neat labels: "utensils," "silverware," "coffee supplies," "potholders." The bathrooms were decorated with matching towels and rugs in various shades of forest green for the upstairs and dusky rose for the downstairs.

I had only cleaned the house once before, so my memory of which towel and rug set belonged to which bathroom was fuzzy. The owners, a Vancouver-based couple, had emailed me specific instructions regarding towel sets, the number of soaps and travel-sized shampoos that belonged in each bathroom, and how the hand towels should be folded.

Squinting at my phone, I scrolled through my emails. "Okay, girls... why don't you start with the rugs. Grab all the rugs and shake them outside."

Sighing deeply, Annika and Mia rolled their eyes, inserted their earbuds and dispersed throughout the house. I clicked on my podcast app and started listening to NPR's *This American Life*. Five minutes later, they were back. "What now?"

"Bathrooms. Go clean the bathrooms."

"How?" They collapsed on floor, feigning exhaustion.

"What do you mean, how?"

"Where's the cleaning stuff?"

"I showed you. Downstairs in that closet by the left door, behind the... Oh, never mind." Irritated, I stomped downstairs. "Here." I shoved the basket into Annika's hands.

"What do I do first?"

I bit my lip. This was supposed to be fun. This was bonding time. "Start with the bowl part. Squirt some of this in there."

The rest of the afternoon passed quickly. Every five minutes one of them appeared with a question that seemed unbelievably obtuse. As I reached into the dryer to grab the last load of laundry, I heard a familiar, "Mom!"

"What?!"

"Where do the rugs go?"

"Where you found them!"

Silence. I wiped the sweat from my forehead and waited.

"We don't know where we found them."

Shit.

◆◆◆◆

Three days later, I got a text from the homeowner. My new husband, Todd, and I were in Seattle at Dimitriou's Jazz Alley.

> We have a problem! The upstairs bathroom had dark green towels with the light green bathmat, which goes as I explained, in the downstairs bathroom. The downstairs bathroom had three rose hand towels, not four...???The side bathroom had a different color altogether, and I cannot comprehend how every rug in the entire house has ended up in a different location. I am baffled. CALL ME.

I tried to be cool. He owned the house. If he really cared which towel sets went in which bathroom, that was fine. But when I called him the next morning, he was irate. I couldn't tell whether it bothered me more that a grown man was lecturing me on the location of different colored hand towels, or that I—as a forty-two-year-old college professor and mother of two—was taking it.

I told my friends Heather and Sarah about the incident.

"But Julie, you have a PhD!" Sarah paused from rinsing salad greens in the sink and shook her head.

"That's exactly the point." I took a sip of water. "It shouldn't matter."

"I suppose you're right."

"Besides, he doesn't know."

"It's kind of like a social experiment." Heather plucked a string on her guitar. "Like that book…"

"*Nickel and Dimed*?"

"Yeah, Barbara Ehrenreich. You're going undercover as a housecleaner."

"Except *The New York Times* didn't send me."

◆◆◆◆

The initial text was followed by three emails and fourteen pictures of each bathroom, bedroom, and rug in the house—all in their proper place with the appropriate towels.

I wondered why the owners didn't just have the same colored towels for the entire house. Every time I cleaned it took me an extra hour to run back and forth from the basement to the third floor to double-check whether I had the right towels for the four different bathrooms. The owner was idiosyncratic to say the least, but it was more than that. Studies show that when people are put in positions of power, they do things they wouldn't normally do. In the famous Stanford Prison Experiment, the make-believe guards punished the make-believe prisoners for minor misdemeanors with psychological abuse. They made them do hundreds of pushups or sit with their faces to the wall. Before the study, they were college students and peers. Philip Zimbardo, the research coordinator, concluded that it's the roles, not our values or beliefs, that determine our behavior.

I'm not saying I was being treated like a prison inmate, but when I submitted my time records and the owner questioned whether it had really taken me five hours to clean, I was astounded. I explained that someone had tracked river sand all over the downstairs floor. I had to sweep, vacuum, and mop, which indeed took an extra hour.

Not possible, he texted back. The house is not on the river.

I figured I knew sand when I saw it. The towels were full of sand too. Obviously, the family had gone to the river and come home with sand on their shoes. Did he think I was lying?

He began to send me needling texts.

> Can you please send a detailed description of cleaning methods used along with your hours?

Okay.

> Can you please resend as a pdf? I absolutely cannot read this.

It was a Word document.

> Can you please confirm that the refrigerators are completely empty and cleaned?

Yes, of course. The refrigerators have been cleaned. The last clients left some beer in the refrigerator. I left it for the next guests?

> Absolutely not. We never leave food in the refrigerators.

But… beer?

I finally broke down and mentioned via text that I, too, had a second home—in Hawai'i, which I rent out as well. My mother cleans it. I tried to imagine telling Mom which towels to put in the bathroom. I tried to imagine caring. I couldn't.

I suppose I texted him this in order to set the record straight, just a little. Although I wanted to go along as though it didn't matter who I was in other areas of my life, I was starting to lose sleep over the bathmats. Did I put the light green with the rose towels or the dark green? Did I roll them or fold them? The fact that I was a college professor, had a book coming out, and owned two houses shouldn't matter. But it did. In fact, it made it worse.

◆◆◆◆

The other house I cleaned was a much older house just outside Winthrop. It was a party house. Groups of ten to fifteen people rented it for a weekend. They left behind trash cans full of beer bottles, wrapping paper, pizza boxes—and once, seven fifty-gallon garbage cans full of something that emitted a fetid odor. I had to take a special trip to the dump in my Toyota Highlander.

Overall, I enjoyed cleaning this house. Mia, my youngest daughter, met me after school to help clean. After a half-hearted attempt to fold towels or wipe down the refrigerator, she'd wander down to the bakery for a snack. When she came back, she watched me mop the floors. Sometimes she played music from her playlist. I hoped she was benefitting from my little lectures on how to clean a house from top to bottom, starting with the beds and ending with the floors.

"See, Mia? If you vacuum your way out of a room, you don't leave any tracks. Isn't that cool?"

"Mmhmm." She'd smile vaguely, munching on a bagel. "What do you want to hear next, Mom?"

Midway through the summer, the owners called and wanted to meet in person. They lived near Portland and planned to stay for two weeks in July. We decided to meet at three in the afternoon, which gave me enough time for a trail run before the meeting. When I got back to my car at the trailhead, I realized I was out of service and running late. I didn't want to show up in shorts and a sports bra, so I quickly changed clothes in the car and hightailed it back to Winthrop.

Smoothing my hair into a ponytail, I knocked on the screen door. The owners answered with big smiles. They looked to be in their mid-fifties. The man wore a tight black tank top with some graphics I couldn't decipher. The woman, pleasantly heavyset, had on jean shorts and a spaghetti strap top. Her arms were covered with tattoos.

"Julie?" The woman shook my hand.

"You come from the pass?" The man glanced at my legs, which were covered in dust.

"Yeah. Really nice up there."

"Want some water?"

"Yes, please." I was parched.

We went through the house together. The woman explained how she liked the beds made, how the towels should be folded, and where the soaps should sit. Dutifully, I made notes and chatted about Winthrop, tourism, and the summer season. They mentioned that their son was graduating from Gonzaga University.

"I did my undergraduate there," I offered.

"Wow, no kidding!"

"Yeah, I'm actually doing a book event there in a couple months." I don't know why I said this. Even as the words slipped out of my mouth, I mentally kicked myself. I had planned not to tell them anything about my other life. Not only did I know somehow that they wouldn't like it, but I didn't want to be that person who has to name-drop credentials.

"Really? You have a book coming out?"

"I do."

"What's it about?"

"It's kind of a memoir, coming-of-age thing in Nepal." Stop talking, Julie. Stop talking!

"Wow. That's interesting. Honey, we should buy a copy for Henry."

"You're right. He would really be interested in that."

Two hours later when I finally extricated myself from the conversation, we hugged goodbye. I felt like we were old friends.

"So good to meet you finally!"

"Oh, my goodness... yes! You too!"

A week later I received a voicemail.

> Yes, hi, Julie, this is Cheryl. We won't be needing your services any longer. Uhmm, yeah. We just, you know. It's just not going to work out. You can return the keys to the reservation service as soon as possible. Okay, bye.

I listened to it again. "But they loved me!" I told my husband. "I know they did. We had a great conversation. There was nothing wrong with the house. They said it looked beautiful."

"Well, sweetie... I don't know. Do you want to call them?"

I shook my head. "I just can't figure it out. Why would they fire me in mid-summer? What did I do?"

I fumed about it all evening. Although I hated to admit it, I was hurt—and embarrassed. I'd never been fired from any job in my life. I couldn't believe that they had just let me go. I mean, it was a *housecleaning job*... are you kidding? I wanted to tell that woman that I had a PhD. I owned two houses. I was a college professor.

Maybe that was the problem.

> Hi, Cheryl. Yeah, this is Julie. I was just calling to see if there was anything I did or didn't do with the house. I mean, that's fine, but I am a little surprised. Can we chat about this?

No phone call. Just a text. *Please return your keys.*

Was it the trail running? Was it the book? Was it the pillows on the bed?

I ruminated over it for weeks. Finally, I chalked it up to part of my sociological experiment. I will never know exactly why Cheryl fired me, but I think I can guess. People are comfortable when the social order is maintained.

Housecleaners are women. In eastern Washington, they are usually Latina. Housecleaners don't make a lot of money, and they don't have PhDs. They don't write books. Maybe if I'd been twenty-five and a single mom, I would have kept the job. I had broken a cardinal rule. I was over-classed for this job, and that wasn't acceptable.

◆ ◆ ◆ ◆

I continued to clean the Mazama house. Every Monday and sometimes again on Thursdays, the girls and I drove up to Mazama to clean. We played music, stripped the beds, mopped the floors, and scrubbed the bathrooms. The girls got better at cleaning, and we developed a system. We did everything but the floors. Then, while the laundry was drying, we went to the bakery in Mazama for lunch. Sometimes we did a trail run and then lunch. When it was too hot, we took our sandwiches and pastries to the river. I loved our little routine and was sad when the girls started school in September, and I had to clean alone.

By then, I had a new job as Director of Programs for a local non-profit. Now I really didn't need the work, but I was torn. It was good money. It was easy. I got to run on the trails in Mazama.

But I couldn't tell the people I worked with that I cleaned houses on the side. I worried they would find out.

My coworker Craig lived near Pine Forest with his husband George. Their house had been featured in the local Home Tour, and they had a housecleaner.

"I don't know what we'd do without our cleaner." Craig glanced over from his computer screen. He had one of those desks that you can lower or raise. Now he raised it and stood. "I mean, the dog hair alone!"

I sighed. The night before, I'd gone downstairs to say goodnight to Annika and Mia and mistakenly walked into their bathroom. What a sight. Hadn't they learned anything from cleaning all summer?

"Well, I ended up cleaning three bathrooms at eleven last night," I announced grimly. "I think I'm the only person in the house who picks anything up, ever. I mean really. Ever."

"You should get a housecleaner. I can give you mine's number."

I considered telling Craig that I was a housecleaner. We shared all kinds of things about our lives, and yes—we were obviously in different social classes. He and George planned to retire in Europe the following year and had just spent three weeks looking at villas in the Italian Alps. But Craig was also down-to-earth. He admitted his privilege. "George makes an obscene amount of money for what he does. And I climbed the ladder at Amazon, so this is sort of retirement."

I liked Craig. I liked George, too. I loved hearing about their daily interactions. The most recent conflict involved a new toothbrush head that Craig had purchased. Their exchanges occurred over text, and as Craig's officemate, I was privy to every new ding from his phone.

Craig shook his head and sighed dramatically. "From George," he cleared his throat and read. "I tried the new FOREO ISSA 2 Sonic Electric head. Not impressed. Am looking for the ISSA 1."

Toothbrush heads. I wanted to fight over toothbrush heads. My husband and I fought over things like his children and my daughters, who constantly acted snarky to him. Combining a blended family with five teenage daughters was complicated, to say the least. Toothbrush heads meant that you didn't really have any problems. Or at least—not *my* kind of problems.

"But anyway, back to cleaning." Craig adjusted his glasses. "Do you want her number?"

I've never felt like I was too good for domestic labor. In the Sociology of Women class I teach, we talk about global trends where first-world women offload their domestic chores onto third-world women. Moms in L.A. hire Latina women to raise their children and clean their houses while Latino men maintain their swimming pools and gardens. All the while, their time is freed up for more creative endeavors, like book clubs, art, or lunching with friends and shopping.

I always felt uncomfortable with this. Even if you worked at a prestigious law firm—or, let's say, in my fantasy world, a university—why should your time be more valuable than another's? Rural Washington State is certainly not New York City or Los Angeles, but even here the differences in class are stark. A few years ago, I had a student who moved to Washington from Mexico, leaving behind two small children. She worked as a nanny by day and in the orchards at night.

"How did you stand it?" I asked.

"I didn't. I cried every night for five years. It almost killed me."

While her children lived with a relative in Mexico, she spent her days raising someone else's children, reading to them in Spanish, cooking them food, taking them to the park. I know many people accept this as a fact of life. Maybe they don't see anything wrong with it.

In fact, as I sat there staring at my computer screen, the thought of hiring a housecleaner sounded more and more like a good idea. Spotless floors when I got home. Sparkling windows. Laundry folded. Maybe a gardener, too. All my perennials weeded and staked. The lawns—*wait a minute*.

What was I thinking? *I am a housecleaner.*

◆◆◆◆

A couple months later, I received a text from the owner of the Mazama house. I had told him that I would be in Hawai'i over Christmas. Originally, he had said that would be fine. Now:

> Julie, we will not be needing your services any longer. It is quite unacceptable for a housecleaner to be gone during one of the busiest seasons of the year. This will not work for us.

Well, good, I thought. Because I was going to quit anyway. But again, it rankled. I would much rather have quit both houses than been... let go. Fired. It was like being rejected. Divorced.

I learned an important lesson during my housecleaning stint at forty-two years old. Even when you think you can buck the system, when you think you're above it intellectually or morally, you're not. I was sure that cleaning houses at age forty-two would feel different than it did at twenty. When I was twenty, I felt powerless, but it's hard to feel equal to someone when you're on your hands and knees scrubbing their floor. It wasn't the cleaning I disliked, but the way the role made me feel, like I wasn't a person. I was a cleaner.

When I got the text, I fantasized about meeting the owner at a fundraising soiree for the non-profit where I worked. There would be good wine and cheese plates, organic crackers, music in the background.

Someone would introduce us. "Oh, Steve… you know Julie, here. She's the Director of Programs."

"Hello, Steve. Nice to meet you." I would shake his hand and smile.

A tiny frown would crease his forehead. I would look familiar. He would wonder where he'd seen me before. He'd shake his head and smile. He'd say, "Lovely to meet you, Julie. Tell me about yourself."

Puckett Creek

I was a strange kid. Junior high was not a great time for me. I don't know if it's a great time for anyone, but it was definitely a low point in my life.

I didn't have much going on in junior high. I didn't do sports because we lived too far from school. We had church and youth group, but that was my parents' thing. I read a lot of books and lived mostly in my head until I discovered Puckett Creek.

Puckett Creek was an abandoned homestead about three miles from our house. Every day after school, I'd change clothes, grab an apple, and head outside. I wasn't supposed to go there. Puckett Creek ran through a rancher's land, and he had specifically said we could not go on his property. We'd asked permission when we first moved to the farm.

"Nope." He spat a stream of brown tobacco juice into the day lilies by his house.

"Well, okay, then." My dad glanced at my sister and me. This was not going the way he'd planned. We had bought horses that year, and Dad was hoping for permission to ride on this man's property, which lay adjacent to our farm.

"Nope, Dave. It's Dave, right?" The rancher grinned. "I never give anyone permission to go on my land. It's a slippery slope, ain't it? If I give you permission, then someone else wants permission, and on and on. You can see how it is."

I could see how it was. I could see that my only hope of one day becoming a land baron like him was to marry his son, who was a few years older than my sister. At twelve years old, this seemed like a long way off, but I kept it in the back of my mind. Marrying a rancher with a lot of land seemed like a good idea.

In the meantime, Puckett Creek became my obsession. I'd hike the two miles up the dirt road until it dead-ended at the green gate. Ignoring the "No Trespassing" signs, I'd slip under the fence, then run like mad. Once out of sight, I'd slow down. Puckett Creek was an underground spring that bubbled up in a private, empty valley. Aspens had long since colonized the creek bed, along with alders and a few cottonwoods. To get to the homestead on the other side, I had to pick my way through a wetland of mud and cattails and thick underbrush. An abandoned car from the 1930s had lodged in the mud and turned brown with rust. Various animals made their nests in this car—often squirrels and raccoons, but once I saw a porcupine in the backseat.

The woods smelled gamey and wild. I always looked for fresh tracks in the mud. I saw cougar, bobcat, coyote, bear, and raccoon tracks. I grew to recognize their scent along with their tracks. I fancied that I could sense when an animal had just left or when it was coming.

Once I made it through the wetland, I broke out into what I called my Secret Valley.

It was wide and empty with a dark fringe of forest on one end and the remains of a burned-down homestead on the other. An enormous lilac bush grew near the ruin, and as winter faded, great purple irises bloomed in clumps around the stone foundation.

When I first discovered the homestead, I was entranced. I wanted to know who had lived there and why it had burned. Since there was no Internet in that day, I made up my own stories about the place. I decided there must have been a beautiful young woman who had moved out West to be with her handsome husband. I named the woman Ellie because it was my favorite name. I gave her long brown hair. She wore blue, gingham dresses and a bonnet, like Laura Ingalls Wilder. She was madly in love with her husband, who didn't have a name. Vaguely, I imagined he would look like a version of the rancher's son—blond hair, blue eyes, well-built. He was always a bit fuzzy in my mind, as I was only twelve. Eventually, I made the husband go away because the narratives didn't fit with him around. I shipped him off to war. Now Ellie lived alone with her small child, a little girl. Ellie had a hard life. She had to draw water from the creek and farm the fields by hand. She made preserves from the wild plums in the wood, and she baked bread over her brick oven. She lived through the hot summers and long winters. She and her little girl—I named the girl Margaret—sat under the aspen trees and watched sunsets from the hill. Music even played in my mind, the theme song from *Anne of Green Gables*. Sometimes the scenes were so touching they brought tears to my eyes.

I spent hours wandering around the meadow, picking flowers and pretending that I was Ellie. If I'd been a little weirder, or braver, I would have smuggled a homestead dress and bonnet with me so I could really play out my fantasy. As it was, I was a little embarrassed, especially as I grew older.

I loved my Secret Valley. It was hot in the summer and there were a lot of snakes. My favorite seasons were spring and fall. I went in the winter, too, on skis, but it was hard to climb over the fence with skis. In places, the snow drifted past my waist. But in the fall, the aspen leaves turned bright yellow. I'd lie on my back in the field and look up at the canopy of yellow against the blue sky. I breathed in the scent of cottonwoods and the wet, marshy smell of the creek. Leaves spun down in the breeze.

In the spring, I saw a lot of wildlife. Deer, of course, but also coyotes, bobcats, a cougar—that was scary—and bear.

One year, when I was sixteen, I came up with my dog, Copper, and best friend, Liz. We were just about to enter the dark woods before the homestead when we heard a loud crash.

We froze.

Behind me, Liz shifted her feet. "What was that?"

"I don't know." I took a few steps. "Come on."

"Wait!" Liz shook her head. "That sounded big."

"Oh, come on. It's fine."

I glanced back at Liz. Her mouth hung open in a perfectly round O shape. She pointed behind me. I turned, just in time to see a black bear emerge from the trees in full charge. Copper had flushed it out.

The bear headed straight for me.

I hesitated. She was about fifty yards away. Too close to outrun. I'd heard that you were supposed to play dead during a bear attack. Maybe I should lie down.

The bear paused for a moment, then reared up on her hind legs. She pawed the air and snorted. When she came down, I turned and ran. Never had my legs felt so weak or the ground so far away. I felt like I was running in slow motion. My arms pumped at my sides. My knees came up, then down, up and down.

In front of me, Liz screamed, "Run, Julie! Run!"

We ran. I couldn't look back. I was too scared. When we finally made it to the fence, we vaulted over it, tearing our shorts and collapsing on the ground. We glanced behind us.

The bear was gone. So was my dog. Copper had distracted the bear and run off into the creek thickets. We could hear them thrashing around in the undergrowth.

"Copper!" I called for the dog.

"Let's just go, come on." Liz yanked my arm. "Run!"

We ran. We ran all the way to the paved road before we stopped, panting. Our junior prom was that night, and we were supposed to be getting ready. "What about Copper?" I felt terrible for leaving him.

"Let's ask your dad. He'll come back and look for him."

By the time we got home, Copper was limping down the driveway. His tongue hung from his mouth and his hip was dislocated, probably from the bear swatting him. But he was alive. I put my arms around his shaggy head and kissed his nose.

Copper had saved the day.

◆◆◆◆

I learned a lot about animals at Puckett Creek. I learned that snakes hear through vibrations in the ground, so you should stomp your feet to scare them off. A rattlesnake den near the green gate kept me wary, especially in the spring when they liked to come out and lie in the sun.

After the bear episode, I made noise before heading into the woods. Never surprise a bear, especially with cubs. I learned that coyotes hunt in the evening and the morning, as do cougars and most animals. If you don't want to see animals, the afternoon is best. I learned that bucks will actually attack you, especially in the fall when they're in rut and their necks are thick and full. Once, I saw a moose in the woods. His long legs and beard surprised me. Another time, I saw what I thought was a martin or a badger. I couldn't tell, but it ran snarling across my path so fast that I had to jump backwards to avoid stepping on it.

I learned all this and more, largely by myself. Today, kids don't spend hours by themselves in the woods. As a parent, I worry about the girls going anywhere alone, much less the pond or the river. But I know that being alone in wild places is priceless.

I figured stuff out when I was alone up Puckett Creek. My mind reverted to its natural mode—a calm but engaged state that psychologists call mindfulness. Today I take classes and practice meditation to achieve mindfulness, but I think mindfulness happens whenever I spend a few hours outside. Being outside is a full-sensory experience. The temperature, the wind, the sounds, the feeling of mud between your toes. It all works to wake us up to the natural world.

Another thing that happened during those afternoons in the Secret Valley is that I started to get to know myself. It happened naturally. I didn't do this consciously.

The word "consciousness" derives from the Latin word, *conscius*—*con*, meaning together, and *scio*, to know. Originally, it meant to know with oneself, not to know oneself, as we think of it today. Early Latin writings included the term *conscius sibi*, which meant literally, "sharing knowledge with oneself about something." And this is exactly what my mind did when left alone to contemplate the natural world. I began to share bits of knowledge with myself.

Look at the way the grass is matted down there—I wonder if an animal slept here last night. Oh, right. Here's some scat. There's a track. I wonder if I ought to be here right now. And so on.

This kind of knowing made me happier. I saw simple things. Trees, bugs, birds. And I began to make friends with myself.

I think about this now—to know *with oneself* as opposed to knowing yourself. To know with oneself means that there is a self inside to get to know. A self inside that is bigger than me, wiser than me. An older consciousness, an older knowing. Maybe it's from a time before language, when we didn't think in thoughts but through emotions and feelings.

Maybe this is the way animals know. How bucks know it's hunting season and when to stay away from my yard. How dogs know to find their way home. How birds know when to fly south.

As a parent, I have a hard time allowing my daughters the same freedom I had. There's a difference between getting your kid outside to recreate versus letting them roam free. I am guilty of this.

I used to make Mia come skiing with me. I thought it would be fun, and I could get my workout in. We'd suit up in our jackets, gloves, hats, ski boots, and poles. We'd break trail down to the river. By the time I got to the woods, I'd look back to see Mia standing in the field with her head tipped back, staring at the sky. Sometimes she'd be crouched down, messing with something at her feet. Mia always dawdled. She dawdled so much it drove me crazy. If we were hiking, she'd lag behind to look at the moss growing on a tree or to inspect a squirrel's hole or a beetle.

"Come on, Mia!" I'd call.

After the tenth time of having to stop and wait, my patience would run thin. "Get a move on, Mia!" I'd yell.

By that time, neither of us was having fun and the afternoon quickly deteriorated.

◆◆◆◆

"Mia's actually smarter than any of us," my new husband, Todd, said one day as we waited for the umpteenth time.

We were hiking with four of our daughters, and Mia was, of course, way behind. Todd and I stopped to watch as she gazed up at the canopy, looking for something that had caught her attention. She swiveled around, listening. We always said Mia was in her own little world, but that wasn't the case. We were in our own little world.

On this day, Todd and I were fighting about something with the kids. The other girls were off ahead, listening to music and talking about boys. Only Mia was paying attention.

We watched her listen, and then we heard it, too. The low thrumming of a grouse beating his wings against a log. It sounded like an engine starting up from a long way off.

At last she wandered up to us. Ever the teacher, I said, "Did you hear that sound, Mia?"

"Yeah."

"Do you know what it was?"

"Yeah." She looked at me like I was crazy.

I didn't believe her. "What was it?"

"A grouse, Mom. The males do that to attract the females."

Mia knows all kinds of things that I don't know, or didn't know at that age. She can tell the difference between a male and a female tree frog. It's based on the ears and size. She knows that lichen grows on the north side of a tree because it has more shade. She knows that tomato hornworms can be either green or brown, and that the holes I saw yesterday were probably a coyote den, not, as I immediately thought, a wolf den.

"Look at the size, Mom."

Right.

Mia has the kind of mind I wish I had. She doesn't get lost in some grand narrative in her head, and if she were wandering around Puckett Creek today, she probably wouldn't be making up love stories about Ellie and the rancher's son. She'd probably be listening for spotted owls.

I spent a lot of years alone up Puckett Creek. I wish I'd spent more. Today, when I go out for my daily excursions, I bring my phone to track my miles. I still love my time outside. I love the way my mind calms down around mile number three. I love the awareness that rises up in my body. I love the sensation of being fully alive, my heart beating, my legs moving, the wind on my face. The sun. But it's different now. I miss that feeling of spaciousness.

Adults live by time. I schedule everything in my day planner—even time outside. I suppose you could say that I have been domesticated. We all have.

I'd like to think I could still spend three hours doing nothing by the river. But I'd probably get bored. I'd bring a book or my journal. You'd have to tie me to a tree to make me do nothing.

If I could go back to those afternoons up Puckett Creek, I would. I'd get back inside that mind. Quietly alive. Quietly aware. As alive and conscious as the aspen trees. Growing. Wild. Breathing. Awake.

Amenity Migration

I know about amenity migrants because I am one. Also, I earned my PhD in the subject—but mostly I know about it because I live it.

An amenity migrant is someone who moves somewhere for the lifestyle it offers. Other people move for work, family, jobs, or to escape poverty, war, and other natural disasters. Migration scholars call this the push and pull factors. Moving somewhere for a new job or to be near family are *pull* factors. Civil war or crushing poverty are *push* factors. Amenity migrants are atypical because they move for none of these reasons. They move for intangible assets like location, lifestyle, and community.

The perception of place is paramount for the amenity migrant. Their chosen places are beautiful, full of natural amenities. These migrants tend to congregate in areas close to national parks and wilderness, large bodies of water, ski resorts, beach towns, or lake towns. They also tend to group within a certain radius of their original home, a one-day's drive if they're employed or a quick plane ride if they're retired.

Amenity migration is not new. The ancient Greeks opined about the benefits of moving to the mountains for lifestyle, and history is full of movements of people disenchanted with daily life who struck out to join a commune or moved to the countryside for the tranquility and peace it offered. What is new is the number of people who can now afford to do so.

Retirement and the idea of an active old age is a new chapter in human history. Prior to WWII, the average life expectancy for men was fifty-five years, and for women fifty-eight. Medical advances and the economic upturn of the 1980s and 1990s created a generation of retirees with twenty-plus years of life left and the wherewithal to enjoy it. Traditionally, leisure studies and tourism departments focused on retirees because they were the only people who had leisure. Today, however, there is a new class of amenity migrants—remote workers.

Remote workers represent a shift in both lifestyle options and the places they migrate. Golf courses and retirement communities in Arizona give way to rock climbing and Nordic ski communities in Colorado. The retiree is replaced by a forty-something hedge fund manager who phones into the office from his mountain bike. Incoming migrants have one thing in common—they rapidly transform the places they inhabit.

◆◆◆◆

In the Methow Valley—a community of just over 10,000 residents—42 percent of the homes are second homes. While the ratio of second- to full-time homeowners has remained the same for more than twenty years, today's full-time resident population is changing as remote workers move into the community and establish themselves. Rural attitudes like resourcefulness, grit, and determination that shaped the community in the past are shifting. Incoming residents demand more services and are less likely to know how to fix their plumbing or plow their driveways. In places like Mazama, Lost River, or Wolf Creek, nearly 80 percent of the homes are second homes. Instead of homesteader cabins with gritty old-timers, planned developments near Mazama like Chechaquo or the Wilson Ranch are filled with sleek designer homes and urban residents with luxury and electric vehicles.

As I said—I, too, am an amenity migrant. Perhaps not as well-heeled as those in the Methow, but part of the same processes. Five years ago, I bought a tiny house in the former plantation town of Nāʻālehu on the Big Island of Hawaiʻi. My daughter and I spent two weeks the first summer repainting, buying furniture, and planting flowers. It felt exotic. Waking in the morning to doves cooing in the Christmas berry, plucking mangos from the giant trees in the front yard, and watching the sunrise over the ocean from the back lanai—I could scarcely believe my good fortune. Like many people who spent their childhoods in the Methow and later purchased a home there, I had spent years vacationing in Hawaiʻi. Now I had a place of my own.

Over the years, we've visited for Christmas, Thanksgiving, and spring break. Every time I set foot in the door after being gone, I'm struck by the sound of coqui frogs chirping in the dark and rain pattering on the metal roof. It feels like coming home. Every time I leave, it's harder to walk away. I love my house in Hawaiʻi. Like amenity migrants in the Methow Valley, I don't appreciate Hawaiʻi less because I have a home there. I appreciate it more.

I also realize that I'll never totally belong in Hawaiʻi. Not really.

In 2020, when Covid-19 brought hundreds of second homeowners to the Methow, we chose to hunker down in Hawaiʻi. My daughters Annika and Mia homeschooled and worked online. I taught classes and ran the programs at my non-profit, TwispWorks, from the back porch. Annika got a job picking coffee. Mia and her cousin took up skateboarding and surfing.

Nāʻālehu is even more rural than the Methow. Established during the sugar plantation era, the town lies overlooking the ocean, surrounded by ranchland and the Kaʻū Forest Preserve. Giant ficus trees lean over the main street, where tour busses stop at the Punaluʻu Bakery for Portuguese malasadas and ice cream. Across the street are two real estate companies, a now-condemned theatre, a hardware store, the bank, and several churches. Nāʻālehu is about 13 percent white, and most of these are retirees who live in Discovery Harbour, a housing development a couple miles out of town. Like the Methow, the retiree and second-home community in Nāʻālehu feels like it supports the town. It shops local. It reads the Kaʻū newspaper. Volunteers are never lacking at charity events, and, as in the Methow, many migrants find themselves in the curious position of being neither here nor there.

To be an amenity migrant is to be in two worlds. Periodically you dig deeper into one of them. As I write this, I am living once again in Nāʻālehu while my daughter attends Volcano School of Arts and Sciences, an hour away. It's still dark at 6:15 AM when I drop her off at the bus stop. Pickup trucks with dog crates and gun racks in the back idle loudly as sleepy kids with hoodies and earbuds stumble to the bus. They're the children of local families—Portuguese, Filipino, Marshallese, and mostly Hawaiʼian.

After I drop off Mia, I head up the back road behind town and go for a run. From here, you can see the entire coastline, green and glittering in the morning sun. Locals call it the Old Cane Road because it used to connect the sugar cane fields, where workers lived in ethnic camps. In the 1920s, the plantation imported workers from Portugal, China, the Philippines, and Japan. The camps were established according to ethnicity, in part because workers spoke different languages but also to keep them from unionizing. Today, you can see the descendants of these workers in the children who file back and forth from school and the families who fish down at Honu'apo.

From the Old Cane Road, the sun rises above a bank of clouds in a radiant spectacle of pink and orange. It's quiet up here in the mornings. I'm alone except for the occasional pickup truck on its way to the coffee fields in Pahala. After the mill shut down in 1996, over half the residents in this area were unemployed. A decade of poverty ensued with families struggling to make ends meet. Some got jobs at the upscale resorts, more than two hours away. Others commuted to work in Hilo. The remoteness of the region, combined with the loss of the plantation, which sponsored a school, community events, and even the hospital in town, was felt acutely by those who had depended on the plantation for several generations. The social fabric unraveled, and many residents described that time as a period of high crime, alcoholism, and despair. However, all was not lost. As part of their severance package, Ka'ū Sugar gave five acres of leased land to each former employee and encouraged them to plant coffee. A private benefactor built a large-scale roasting facility for macadamia nuts as well as coffee, and over the next two decades Ka'ū coffee established a name for itself. Many former plantation workers became coffee farmers and worked for themselves.

Today, as I jog down the Old Cane Road, I'm surrounded by ranchland and patchy clumps of sugar cane. In the distance, terraced coffee fields dot the green hills, while clouds cling to the dark forests. Nāʻālehu still feels like a plantation town to me, but locals say the area is changing. They talk about the new people they see in town and the way the community doesn't feel the same. I know that I am part of that change. Like amenity migrants in the Methow, I recognize that I hold a position of immense privilege. I'm white. I'm from the mainland. I own a second home and I work remotely. I am not tied financially to this rural region where people struggle to make a living and the economic disparity between locals and newcomers is growing.

◆◆◆◆

Kaʻū and the Methow are similar in many ways. Both were once rural, agricultural-based communities. Today, both places are heavily reliant on tourism and renowned for their natural beauty. But unlike Kaʻū, which has largely maintained its agricultural roots, the Methow has become an urban oasis of second homes and remote workers in an otherwise rural Okanogan County.

Amenity migration in the Methow is a combination of several events. Originally part of the seasonal homeland of the Methow Indians, the region was opened to white settlement in 1886—only six years after its incorporation into the Columbia Reservation. Miners, trappers, and fur traders found their way to remote mountain regions like Harts Pass and Slate Creek.

Earlier, the Hudson Bay Fur Company had set up an outpost near what is now Pateros, and with the opening of the Methow homesteaders soon followed the early trail from the Columbia River over Benson Creek and into the Methow Valley. Homesteading was an arduous life. Old-timers today still reminisce about the amount of snow that once fell in the winters, the hard-scrabble existence of digging wells by hand, ranching, dairy farming, and subsistence farming.

Towns came and went. Prior to 1920, there were small townships near most of the mines including Azurite, Chancelor, and Barron. The town of Silver, located between Twisp and Carlton, was washed away in the flood of 1948, along with other communities up and down the river. Always a remote region, it did not really open up until plans for a trans-mountain highway over the Cascade Range became concrete in the 1950s. Following an economic slump, community leaders began to lobby for a road to transport hay and other agricultural goods to markets on the west side of the Cascade mountains. The road would finally materialize in 1972.

By then, as part of the federal Wilderness Act of 1962, most of the land surrounding the Methow Valley had been turned into national parks or wilderness areas such as the North Cascades National Park and Stephen Mather Wilderness, as well as the Pasayten, Glacier Peak, and Chelan Sawtooth Wildernesses. When the North Cascades Highway opened, the Methow Valley was surrounded by one of the largest areas of public land in the United States. This designation had a profound effect on the Methow's economy, turning it into a tourism and outdoor recreation destination almost overnight.

Plans for a downhill ski resort by the Aspen Corporation quickly ensued, and a land rush in Mazama and Early Winters began, which can still be seen in the number of vacation and second homes in the upper valley. The ski resort plan was highly divisive. Some locals wanted jobs and a way for their kids to stay in the valley. Newer residents fell on both sides of the development divide, depending on what brought them to the Methow in the first place. Some came from Aspen, Colorado, hoping to get in before the land rush. Others were urban refugees, fleeing development and the cities from which they came. While the ski resort plans were finally put to rest in 2001, the resulting factions for and against development linger in the community today. Watchdog groups and environmental activists maintain a strong presence in the Methow and oppose many land use and zoning proposals from the rest of Okanogan County. While the Methow is largely corporation-free, it has become a recreation center and bedroom community for Seattle-based second homeowners and remote workers. Instead of large-scale development like a ski resort, the valley has been divided and subdivided into enclaves of second homes. Construction and land sales are the biggest industries in the Methow, not tourism.

◆◆◆◆

The first time I heard the words *amenity migrant*, I was struck by the simplicity of one term that summed up the processes I had witnessed most of my life. The biggest difference between an amenity migrant and any other kind of migrant is money. Amenity migrants are not tied to jobs. They can do what they like. They have free time. Lifestyle, an amorphous concept, becomes the new priority, shaping communities by the things the newcomers buy, the activities they choose, the books they read, the values they bring, and even by the names of the places they transform.

Several years ago, I came across a letter to the editor in the *Methow Valley News*, the local weekly newspaper. An older, local woman was writing in because the road on which she and her family had lived for generations was finally given a name. Unbeknownst to her, some new residents had decided to call it *Nanasu*, a Sanskrit word meaning, "when dreams come true." Understandably, the woman felt like the road should have been named after her family and was outraged that she had not been consulted. Place names have long been symbols of the relationship between colonizers and the colonized.

Native American place names like *Twisp*, which means "yellow jacket," or the *Met-whu* (literally, low-lying valley with blunt hills all around) were based on geographic descriptors of the landscape. For example, the Methow River was *Buttlemuleemauch*, or "salmon falls river," and Chelan was *Tsill-ane*, or "deep water." These original place names were quickly replaced by homesteader family names (Thurlow, Libby, Williams) or the names of animals commonly found there (Cub Creek, Wolf Creek, and Eagle or Buck lakes). Today, new housing developments and roads are named after obscure references like Nanasu and *Chechaquo* (which means newcomer to the land), or Saw Whet Lane after the smallest owl species in North America. Places names are significant because they symbolize the transformation of place. Naming a road after a Sanskrit term or a reference to Jack London (as in Chechaquo) symbolizes a break with the past and a nod to more esoteric or intellectual sensibilities. It's a way to separate the old from the new. It's part of the process of "othering."

Sociologists like to talk about "othering" as a way to highlight how social identities are contested. Othering works both ways—the person with more power or prestige works to separate themselves from someone with less status.

Likewise, people with lower status often use slang, code words, or humor to keep the upper class out.

I know about othering. Several years ago, I was invited to a dinner party at a friend's house. Guests were all amenity migrants, and many held professional jobs and advanced degrees. By the time I arrived, everyone was seated around the table talking animatedly. I found a place just as the host decided to have everyone introduce the person next to them by telling a story. This was problematic. I wasn't really friends with these women. I didn't know any stories about them.

I listened as one by one the women shared an estimable anecdote about the person next to them. One woman had bravely accomplished a thirty-mile trail run, even though she had a cold. Another couple had met at their children's private school in Seattle before ending up in the Methow—surprise! By the time the stories got to me, I was cringing. The woman on my left had moved here ten years ago. She worked for a popular non-profit and was an avid trail runner. Smiling, she took a sip from her glass.

"I first met Julie the summer I was doing ecology studies for my graduate degree. She and her husband ran the Grubstake."

I could feel my face flush.

"You know, I was so hungry between field studies, I would go to the Grubstake for lunch. Julie made the best sandwiches. They were on that special bread—what was it?" She turned to me.

"Nine-grain. It was the nine-grain bread."

"Yes, anyway, Julie is a great sandwich maker."

Everyone nodded politely, waiting for the punchline. But that was it. I was a sandwich maker. The other women were athletes, mothers, and professionals from good schools. Their stories linked their similar class and backgrounds, while I was the local color—the other.

◆◆◆◆

I've thought about this often over the years—the need to define oneself as either like or unlike someone else.

This social referencing is a dance of power. Most of us negotiate our identities to best serve the situation. When it behooves me to act like a local, I do. When it's in my interest to promote my travel or education, I do.

Perhaps one of the conflicts between "locals" and "newcomers" is based on social referencing. In traditional societies, social referencing was based on family. Your last name, where you were born, the land you grew up on, the people to whom you were related—these were the references that framed your identity within the group. In modern societies, grouping is based on like-minded people instead of families. Sociologists call these reference groups. Reference groups are people with similar values, tastes, lifestyles, and hobbies. In communities with high levels of amenity migration, reference groups become the social glue that holds the community together.

In the Methow, the transition from a kinship-based system to a reference-group system occurred over the last two generations, leaving behind those who relied on family for their social identifiers. Today's amenity migrants are linked around common recreational activities. Nordic skiing, mountain biking, trail running, private schools, and serving on the boards of the numerous non-profits have become the new social fabric. Local families find themselves largely outside these systems. While locals can certainly ski, serve on boards, and mountain bike, they do so without the background or prestige of an ivy-league education or financial success.

Grouping in the Methow can be seen geographically. According to Okanogan County data, 80 percent of the houses in Mazama and Lost River are second homes, while only 20 percent of Twisp's houses are second homes. Most incoming migrants would rather be on the Methow Trails system than anywhere else. Home values decrease south of Winthrop, and especially south of Twisp. The result is readily identifiable geographic groupings of people from similar socioeconomic classes, even in such a small valley as this. When people look at their neighbors, they look like them, speak like them, act like them, and believe like them—and sometimes it looks like the same community they left in Seattle.

◆◆◆◆

Here, on the Big Island of Hawai'i, grouping is a little more complicated. Local kids live in Nā'ālehu or Pahala or the housing development called Green Sands. Mark Twain, where we live, is considered more local than neighboring Discovery Harbour, but less local than Green Sands. You can tell a local community by the number of rooster houses with their tiny teepee-shaped roofs that keep off the rain, and by the dogs. While cockfighting is technically illegal in Hawai'i, it's still the most popular weekend activity, and dogs are kept in metal crates specifically for pig hunting.

In Hawai'i, locals and *haoles*—the term for white people—coexist despite their differences, which are vast. While ethnic integration is a hotly contested topic in academic literature, throughout most of rural Hawai'i people talk about living with *aloha*. Aloha is a way of living and treating each other with love and respect. Critics of the idea say that living with aloha was an ideology rooted in the plantation era when multi-ethnic groups had to get along. Hawai'ian pidgin, the local dialect, emerged along with aloha as an ethos to keep people working for the plantation and enslaved to poverty.

I'm sure there may be some element of truth to this critique, but in Ka'ū, if someone says, "Aloha," they mean it. It's never taken lightly. While the state of Hawai'i passed the Aloha Spirit Law in 1986, which mandated that state officials and government workers treat the public with respect, the ethos has long been embedded in rural culture. It's practiced through daily living, particularly outside the tourist areas. In fact, tourists are shockingly ignorant of the aloha spirit with which they are treated. The opposite of aloha has become synonymous with the term *haole*, which, when juxtaposed with aloha, refers to the brash, insensitive culture of mainlanders and other outsiders.

Here in Nā'ālehu, amenity migrants or newer residents learn to slow down and adapt to the islands, rather than bringing their mainland values with them. Perhaps it's this quality that lies in contrast to the Methow. Maybe moving to the Methow thirty years ago might have been like moving to Nā'ālehu today. Thirty years ago, when someone moved to the Methow they were in for a culture shock. Long winters, hot summers, and few amenities were the norm, not the exception. From snowplowing to splitting wood to planting your first tomato starts, these activities were more than chores. They were cultural markers that defined what it was to live in the Methow. Locals used to say with a certain amount of glee that, "Most people wouldn't last the first winter." It was this rubric that defined our valley, even a mere generation ago. Today, amenity migrants don't have to suffer through the long winters. They can commute back to their homes in Seattle or take a long vacation. High-speed Internet has tempered the remoteness, and private jets ensure that wealthy residents can come and go as often as they like.

For many people, the connection to the land was what made the Methow special. Today, this is changing. People are connected to the landscape through recreation, not utility. And for better or worse, amenity migrants are becoming the new Methow Valley. The local residents, who used to show up at community events and contribute what they could, show up less and less. Their stories are obsolete. Their politics seem provincial. The rural culture they embraced is being transformed into a semi-urban culture based on affluence and athleticism.

This change is not all bad. Drive anywhere in the rest of eastern Washington and you'll see communities that got left behind and stayed that way. Towns like Omak or Okanogan, where I teach at Wenatchee Valley College, are a mere thirty-five miles away, but it might as well be a different country. My students are a mix of Latinx and members of the Colville Confederated tribe, whose median annual income is $39,000. Throughout the region, 30 percent of the population lives below the federal poverty level, and an estimated 400 to 500 families are homeless.

Yet even these demographics don't manage to paint the real picture. Main street in Okanogan is a wasteland of boarded-up storefronts interspersed with non-profits, a gas station, and a tire center advertising Bibles for sale. I'm well aware that without amenity migration, the Methow Valley could look like Okanogan.

Ironically, the new master plan for Okanogan County

Tourism Council recommends encouraging amenity migration as a way to increase the county's wealth.

◆◆◆◆

If the cost of gentrification is a few more coffee shops and urban values, maybe it's a good thing. Here in Hawai'i, I'm acutely aware of the color of my skin, my remote income, and the fact that I have two homes. But there's something about the culture here that resists change by outsiders like me. The deep localism that keeps the extended kinship system intact in Hawai'i is rooted in a connection with the land, but it's also rooted in families getting together, in barbeques down at Honu'apo, in fishing and hunting pigs. There's power in this connection. Kids are proud of being from the region. They're proud of their family name and being related to hundreds of people all over the Islands. People like me come and go, leaving the local community strangely untouched. Either you adapt to the existing culture, or you don't stay.

I'd like to think that the juxtaposition of being a local in the Methow Valley and an amenity migrant here in Hawai'i gives me a better perspective than most, but I don't know. Running down the Old Cane Road in the morning sun, I wave at the coffee pickers and keep going. I'm not a local here, and I might never belong. But sometimes I like the feeling of being an outsider. There's freedom in not belonging, and an expansiveness I don't have in the Methow. I've loved the North Cascades since I was a child, but sometimes—and this morning is one of those times—I'm so glad to be alive on this planet, I feel like I belong everywhere.

Summer at the End of the World

It started with a film of clouds and a bit of wind. This was strange. Sunny sky after sunny sky had melted into 103-degree days for weeks on end. Now it was July. Up Libby Creek, we bought a stock tank for the girls to swim in because the summer was so hot. They floated on their backs all afternoon, watching the sky. By evening, the wind picked up and thunder rumbled in the mountains.

"Do you think there'll be fires, Mom?" At eleven years old, Annika worried about everything.

"No, honey." I smoothed a strand of hair away from her face and glanced at the sky. "It's far away. It'll be fine."

I hoped it would be fine. It was one of the driest summers we could remember.

The house was four miles up Libby Creek. From the wrap-around porch you could look out and see walls of green in every direction. To the north was Lookout Mountain, to the east Smith Ridge, to the west Chicamun Ridge, and to the south you could just see a half-mile down the creek where the sky came together over Hornet Draw. We were surrounded by heavily forested mountains on all sides.

In the winter, the snow piled deep in drifts and frosted the ponderosa pines with mounds of marshmallow white. Our log cabin tucked between two thousand-foot ridges looked like a Swiss fairy tale. In the summer, however, the arrowleaf balsamroot turned brown and withered. It crackled along the forest floor when you walked, and heat radiated from the carpet of needles like a combustion engine waiting to explode. Every summer during fire season we peered up at the tops of the ridges, always scanning for a plume of smoke.

There was only one road down the creek. Although we never spoke of it, we all knew that Libby Creek was a firetrap. If you had to get out, you'd better not be walking.

By 9 PM, we heard that a fire had started near Stokes Road in Carlton. That was pretty far away, four miles and across the river. Another had started up French Creek, and a couple more up near Winthrop. As I opened the windows and tucked the girls into bed, I listened for the drone of spotter planes. *At least they're putting them out.*

The next morning, we awoke to the acrid scent of charred trees. Over breakfast, I read on Facebook that the lightning strike on Stokes Road had metastasized into 1,000 acres. All day, the girls and I watched the sky while we made cookies, cleaned house, and picked beets from the garden.

In the evening we saw the glow in the night sky towards Carlton.

"Let's go see it." Kenny finished his beer and stood up.

"Why?" I was putting dishes away. It was 9:30, but too hot to sleep.

"For fun. The girls should see it."

We piled into the truck and drove down the creek. As we came around the corner above the valley floor, I caught my breath. The hillside across the river glowed like a city of embers. It looked like Los Angeles from an airplane. A million twinkling lights, exploding in the darkness. We turned down to the swimming hole. Neighbors stood gathered on the beach.

"Hey, Paul."

"Hey, Ken. Hi, Julie." His face was somber. "Did you hear the Smith house burned?"

"No." My throat felt tight.

Another guy and his wife spoke up. "Yeah, they say Pat's house is next. Someone helped them get out."

"No shit." Ken shook his head.

"Damned lightning."

"Yep."

Everyone fell silent.

The girls were afraid. They wanted to go home. Mia, eight years old, gripped my hand. "Don't go, Mommy," she said, as I waded out to the dark water.

"I'm right here." I floated on my back. "See? It feels nice. Do you want to come in?"

"No." She huddled in my towel on the beach.

We didn't stay long.

"I think it's beautiful," Ken said on the way home.

In the back seat, Annika cried silently. "I think it's awful."

"Me too, honey." I looked out through the dark forest. I hated fire.

In the morning I gathered the girls. What should we do?

We fed the chickens. We made breakfast, cheese toast and homemade jam. Swimming lessons in town. Dinner plans in the evening. Groceries. In the afternoon I drove Annika to a playdate at a friend's house.

From here, we could see another plume billowing up across the valley floor. David, her friend's dad, and I stood in the driveway.

"Last night it was just a little campfire." He rubbed his chin with the back of his hand.

"Did anyone call it in?"

"I think everyone called it in. I'm sure they know about it." He shook his head.

"Why aren't they doing anything?"

"I don't know."

We watched the plume in silence. Already, it was beginning to mushroom, billowing out into the crystalline sky like an inkblot in water.

"I'll have Ken pick up Annika on his way home."

"Sounds good. We'll go swimming."

"Bye."

When I got home the house was quiet. Mia had gone to the river with her cousins.

Dinner, I thought. What shall I make for dinner? Our friends Tom and Jessica were supposed to be coming, but I hadn't heard from them. I couldn't concentrate. I checked the clock—4 PM, plenty of time for dinner.

Flowers. I'll pick flowers.

Barefoot, I walked out to the garden and snipped Shasta daisies and the last of the roses. I arranged them on the dining room table, then went to take the clothes off the line. They were stiff and starchy, the white tops, shorts, t-shirts, socks, and underwear. I hated laundry. There were too many sizes to match up. Mia's tiny shirts, Annika's socks. Ken's work pants. I gave up and threw the clothes into the basket.

Outside, the late afternoon sun filtered through the smoky, sepia-toned sky like an old photograph. Something landed on my arm. I brushed it off. A charred pine needle. Another. I looked up at the sky. Blackened needles and bits of ash drifted down. The back porch was covered.

I went to get the broom to sweep it off. I flipped the light switch in the kitchen. Nothing. The power was out. Damn.

I reached for the phone. Nothing. Walked back outside. More ash and needles raining from the sky. Where was the fire? I went for my purse. Cell phone. No reception. A text from my sister, who lived across the road.

> Where r u? Going down to see where the fire is.

K, I texted back. *LMK.*

I finished taking the laundry down and set the basket inside. I picked up the phone to text Tom to tell him we didn't have power for dinner. Maybe we could grill. I should text Ken and tell him to pick up ice on the way home.

The cell phone rang. My sister.

"Jenn? Jenn? I can't hear you..."

Her voice, tiny and distant, crackled through the line. "Julie… listen to me very carefully. We're at a level three evacuation. You need to get in the car and get down right now."

"We're what?" I said, in disbelief and irritation.

"Get in the car," she said. "Get out now!"

I would hear those words again and again over the next few weeks. They would reverberate through my mind, and I would smell the scent of old, stale smoke. I would taste it in my mouth, the taste of bitter ash and helplessness and fear.

I looked at the sky. Silence. Everything was completely still.

I stuffed the cell phone in my purse, grabbed my car keys. I looked around. What to take? The dog, of course. The pregnant cat. The girls had made a birthing box out of the dog crate and decorated it with messages like, "Congratulations, Creamy!" and "It's a boy," "It's a girl!" I stuffed the cat into the crate, my hands shaking. The latch wouldn't close. Forget it. The cat meowed plaintively, hot and terrified.

I ran to the car, threw the dog and the crate in the back. *My sweater*, I thought, *I want the new brown sweater I just bought.* I hadn't even worn it yet. I reached for the sweater. Clothes for tonight? Jammies? Underwear? I couldn't think. From my purse, the phone started buzzing.

Get out, she texted. *Get out now.*

Fuck.

I was sweating, and big sobs rose from my chest. I took one last look at the kitchen. Quiet, dark, peaceful. Everything put away. Cool.

Outside, smoke hung in the air, fresh new smoke, blue, the color of campfires and spring and old jeans and family. I jumped in the car. Gunned the engine. In the yard, Shasta daisies bloomed like fireflies along the garden fence. I could see my roses, columbine, and bee balm. I should pick some lettuce, I thought. Or beets. The girls like beets.

Get out, get out, get out.

I put the clutch in reverse and backed out fast. I was driving then, dust billowing up behind me as I looked back at the front yard. Our old log house, the garden, all the flower beds I'd put in over the years, the wedding I was going to have someday in the front yard with hanging lanterns and white tablecloths. Annika was going to get married in this yard, and maybe Mia.

No.

I drove fast, too fast, sobs coming out of my throat. I heard someone crying. It was me. On the way down, flames licked up the sides of trees, raw orange. There were trucks, fire trucks and Forest Service trucks, and people I knew in fire suits and helmets. A policeman in a car going door to door. I rolled down my window.

"Hi," I said, my voice sounding apologetic. "Do you think I can come back to get anything?"

"If I were you, Ma'am, I'd keep on going." He glanced down. "Stuff is just stuff."

"Right," I said. *But it isn't*, I thought. It's not the stuff, it's the home. My girls. What are they going to do without a home?

On the highway, there were blockades, and my neighbor standing barefoot with her toddler on the side of the road, looking confused. The fire had jumped the river and started up Libby Creek. It was burning down to Pateros, thirty miles away, and no one seemed to know anything.

No one knew what to do or where to go or who to call.

I kept driving. I recognized Brian, a guy I'd gone to high school with. He was a volunteer firefighter. Brian waved at me and nodded.

"It's gonna be okay, Julie." He leaned down to the car window. "Just go. Leave it."

The look on his face was the same as the police officer's. I could read it now—pity. They knew what I didn't. We were all going to lose everything.

I drove to the Carlton Hole, where Mia was swimming with her cousins. They met me on the highway. I grabbed her and scooped her up like a baby, even though her legs dangled past my knees. I pressed my cheek to her forehead and breathed in the smell of river water and sunscreen. Thank God.

That night was the beginning of the end of Libby Creek. I began to think of it as the summer at the end of the world, because that's what it seemed like. The fires combined into one giant, consuming force. It was the largest fire in Washington State history. It raged for three weeks, burning more than 256,000 acres and consuming 353 homes and businesses.

For the next few days, we stayed at a friend's hotel in Winthrop. All the tourists had left. Anyone who had a home in Seattle or friends with a home left. The power was out for the whole valley. Washington Pass closed to east-bound traffic. Highway 153 was closed completely. The power lines had burned. The phone lines were down. Texts worked for the first few days, then Verizon shut down. For three weeks, the Methow was shut off from all outside communication. The only mode of contact was instant messaging on Facebook, which for some reason still worked.

For days, people drove around, wondering what to do. They'd ask each other where the fire was. It was so hard to tell. You couldn't see anything because the smoke was so thick. There was no news, no restaurants, nothing open except Hank's grocery store in Twisp because Hank had a generator. The girls and I, along with the pregnant cat and dog, drove around from place to place. We couldn't settle anywhere. The girls were restless, bored. I was nervous and scared. We spent two nights down in Bridgeport with my aunt so I could check my emails and grade papers online.

One afternoon, the girls and I decided to go back to Libby Creek to check on the chickens. Ken had driven to Burlington to pick up a generator. We'd heard from neighbors that the house was still there. Some people had stayed and refused to leave. My sister was at her house. We drove the back way, thirty miles from Twisp River through Black Pine Lake, because the Libby Creek road was closed, and the National Guard wasn't letting people through. As we turned up our dead-end road below the house, everything looked serene. The trees were still there, the creek sparkled in the sun. Our house looked peaceful. The yard was drying out and my flowers wilted in the sun, but everything was quiet.

The girls and I wandered around together, lost and disoriented.

"What should we do?" Mia asked.

Annika looked at the hills. "Is it safe? Should we leave?"

"Let's pick up your rooms," I said.

We went into the house and changed all the sheets on the beds. We smoothed the wrinkles out and pulled the blankets tight. I picked more flowers and fed them with water from the stock tank. I arranged them everywhere, like you would with a cancer patient. My house *was* a patient. It was going to die, and I felt pity for it. If it's going to burn, I thought, I want it to go clean. Fold, sweep, straighten, put away.

We made a picnic and read stories in the yard. We waited a while before we left. It felt weird to leave your home when it seemed safe. We didn't know where to go this time. And we did this every day until it seemed ridiculous. We were still at a level three evacuation, but gradually, people along the creek came back. We had nowhere else to go.

We came home. By now, there were fire crews from all over the country. The National Guard had taken up residence to discourage looting. The Red Cross distributed soap and water bottles, and offered counseling for what we'd been through. But still, we were at a level three.

I didn't want to stay the night. I couldn't sleep, wondering if the fire was flaring up. You could see it now from the house. Through the trees, you could see dull orange flames during the day, and at night in the dark, you could see trees silently exploding and firebombs erupting like 4th of July fireworks. It made me nervous.

I made Ken promise to spend the night in the bunkhouse at the edge of the property to keep an eye on the fire. I put the girls to bed. Annika had arranged Creamy's crate in her room.

Everything was quiet except the crackle of fire from across the valley.

I awoke at 1 AM from a dead sleep. I sat upright in bed. Something was wrong. I ran to Annika's room and peered out the window. A police car sat at the end of the driveway and a fire truck rumbled quietly in the road. They were coming for us. From under the bed I heard a tiny squeak. Not now, Creamy. Not now. I lay on my belly and shone a flashlight under the bed. Sure enough, there was Creamy with three wet kittens, nursing vigorously. She purred loudly, her eyes wide and unblinking. Kittens. Tonight. And the police were in the driveway.

Barefoot, I grabbed my sweater and ran outside. I knocked on the window of the police car. It was empty. I ran to the fire truck and tried to see inside. A young man stuck his head out.

"Hey there. You live here?" He pointed to the house.

"Yes."

"How many of you are here tonight?"

"There's four of us. Why? What's happening? Where's the fire?"

"It jumped the creek, ma'am. We're just getting a head count of how many people are up here."

"Should we leave?" My voice sounded shrill and panicky.

"It's up to you, ma'am. You're at a level three evacuation."

"Sir." I tried to smooth my wild hair. "I have two little girls asleep and a cat that's having kittens as we speak. If I need to get in the car, I will, but—"

"I'll tell you what, ma'am. I'm stationed here all night. If you need to leave tonight, I'll make sure you get out."

I wanted to kiss that young man. Instead, I started crying. "Thank you. Don't forget. Two little girls. Please come get us."

"I will, ma'am. Go to sleep."

I stumbled back to the house, shaking with terror and gratitude. The man's kindness meant everything. He wasn't going to let us die. I could go to sleep. He promised.

In the morning, there was rain.

I don't know why or how it rained. It wasn't in the forecast, and the Methow is not a place where rain ever arrives unannounced. And it never rains in July. Ever. It felt like a miracle. I tiptoed into Annika's room, where I could see the fire from her window. The fire trucks were still there. I opened the window. The smell of rain swept in, and a cool breeze ruffled the curtains.

We were going to make it. The house wasn't going to die. From under the bed I heard soft mewing.

"Annika, wake up." I shook her gently. "Guess what?"

◆◆◆◆

A month later, there was a divorce.

It happened as quickly as the fires had metastasized that first night after the lightning storm. In retrospect, I suppose it was growing and taking root for years, but the fires had the curious effect of amplifying the process. Like a prism, everything was reflected and re-reflected in a million different angles, and our life fell apart.

I don't remember much of the divorce, but I remember the rain. By the end of September, it started to rain. It rained and rained every day for weeks. All through October it rained, and November too. Mudslides took out houses now, instead of fires, and the roads closed again. But I didn't care. I stood out in the rain, barefoot, at night, listening to the sound of water. Water everywhere, soaking into the earth, splashing on the metal roof, flooding the basement. Nothing had ever sounded so beautiful, and never had I felt so lost. How do we make all those pieces fit, I wondered again and again. Little socks here, big socks there. Dad clothes here, Mom clothes there.

Sometimes things come undone suddenly. Like the reservoir dams up Benson Creek that burst with the first rains. We never did find our way home again. When the smoke had settled, the fires were out and the marriage was gone—and with it the home. And even now, years later, I still wonder where to put things. If you could pick up emotions like you pick up a room, you could put the nice ones on top. You could shake out the resentments, the old stories, the irritations. You could sweep up the crumbs of a marriage and polish the floors of your heart until they shone. You could keep better track of new messes.

The 2014 fires imprinted the Methow's collective memory like an abusive childhood. No one would ever again look at cumulus clouds in the summer and not wonder if it was a fire column. No one would ever hear thunder or dry lightning without checking the weather service and calling their neighbors.

I'd like to say that we learned about community, that the Methow became collectively more compassionate and equitable for its residents. I'm not sure we did. Like my own end-of-the-world summer, I think it made us a bit more desperate. Less naive about what can happen. We lost our innocence that summer.

But perhaps we gained some gratitude.

I'll never forget the firefighter who sat in his truck at the end of our driveway so I could sleep and the rain that greeted me that morning. I am never more grateful than for a summer without fire. Rain in summer is like money in a bank account. I'm grateful we didn't lose our house that night. I'm grateful we got to say goodbye later. I'm grateful we got through the divorce and that the girls are relatively unscathed. I'm grateful for new beginnings and love, and old loves, and goodbyes. I'm grateful my daughters still love cats and that I can still check on them at night. Every day is a gift. Nothing is forever. Nothing is certain.

Sometimes, even now, I go out at night and listen to the rain. I breathe in the clean, sweet scent of wet grass. I think about climate change and our heating planet. I know we've done this to ourselves, and I know it will only get worse. But for this moment, tonight, all I can say is thank you.

Thank you, thank you, thank you.

The Farm

I say that Libby Creek was *one* of my great loves, because eventually I had another.

When a blue-eyed rancher from Montana proposed to me at a hot springs in Hawai'i several years after my divorce, I was smitten. With him. Not his house.

It wasn't completely crazy. He had a farm near Twisp. Our daughters were great friends. But there was one problem. Which one of us would move?

"I can't live in a forest, sweetie."

I paused, wondering how to put it. "But Todd... I'm a girl. I need flower beds. And I like nice tablecloths." This didn't make sense, even to me, but I didn't know how to tell him that his house was a little rough. It wasn't the kind of home where I could imagine arranging my tablecloths and flowers.

Todd's place, as I thought of it back then, was a man's place. The house, built in 1986, was situated on 10 acres of riverfront with views of Mount Gardner to the north and Lookout Mountain to the south. With 150 acres of floodplain and river woodlands surrounding the property, it was certainly a charming location. But the house itself was an odd mixture of eclectic hippie and decades of neglect. Hoping to rent it out for a high price, the previous owners had painted the original Spanish stucco a canary yellow, added some lavender trim to the doors and windows, and covered the living room with a coconut husk flooring. The coconut floor was interesting, but you couldn't clean it—vacuuming and sweeping sucked up fibers, not dirt. After ten years of various renters, the house was in disrepair.

By the time I met Todd, he was in the middle of remodeling the downstairs as a separate living space to rent. He'd replaced the wiring and sheetrock and taken out the coconut flooring, but the house was a work in progress. Most of the last few years, he'd spent building the farm—fencing the upper pasture, then the lower pasture. He planted an acre of blueberries and built a greenhouse, in which he grew tomato and pepper starts. Over the years he had horses, a donkey, pigs, goats, rabbits, and sheep.

My other problem was the sheep. Todd loved his sheep. There were eight ewes and one ram. They were Dorfins, fat-bodied, with short woolly coats and floppy ears. Like a pack of spoiled children, they ruled the property. Literally. They slept in the barn most nights, but every morning they slipped out of their corral and ran free. Sometimes they'd wander onto the neighbor's property or down to the floodplain, but generally, they seemed to know the boundaries of the farm. They'd been fenceless for years.

The sheep liked to hang out in the yard under the shade of an enormous apple tree. Someone had planted the tree before the house was built. Now, it grew wild and formed a canopy with branches draped to the ground.

One afternoon, I stopped by before Todd was home. As I opened the car door, the sheep, dozing under the apple tree, stumbled to their feet. Wandering over, they stared at me with their dull blue eyes. The ram, a stalky fellow with massive curling horns, stomped his tiny hooves and snorted. I started to walk toward the front door. The ram took a step. I hesitated. Certainly, he was friendly. Right? He took another step.

I called Todd.

He chuckled. "Ah, Little Ram won't hurt you. But hold on, yeah, don't get out of the car until I get there. He might charge."

I knew I had to do something about the sheep. How could I grow flower beds and keep a green lawn?

"So, Todd... the sheep."

"What about them?"

"They don't have fences."

"Yeah, they're free range." He laughed. Todd came from a prominent homesteading family in Dillon, Montana. They were sheep ranchers, and his little herd was a symbol of his family's history. I didn't know how this would go.

Eventually, I started putting in flower beds in preparation for the move. First one enormous border in the back yard, then another that looped around behind the apple tree. I started with perennials from the beds up Libby Creek. I'd dig up a carload of starts and drive straight to the farm, where I worked for hours, digging, planting, watering. I transplanted peonies, roses, gooseberries, Echinacea, Salvia, Shasta daisy, and bee balm.

I dug anything that looked squished or overcrowded at Libby Creek. When I exhausted my beds at home, I hit the Walmart in Omak. That spring, I taught anthropology at the college, so I had the perfect excuse to stop by the store before class. I loved strolling around the garden section, picking out bachelor buttons, purple Phlox, Clematis, and orange Gaillardia. The staff at Walmart began to recognize me.

"You again," they'd say. "You must be working on a big project."

I was. I couldn't stop. I wanted flowers and more flowers. I wanted flowers everywhere.

Todd was dubious. "Are you sure you can plant all that?"

I was sure. In fact, I was addicted. The flower fetish lasted for about four years. By then I had planted eighteen trees—maples, a weeping cherry, Japanese lilac, red osier dogwood, hydrangea trees (there is such a thing and it's amazing)—and hundreds, literally hundreds, of perennials. By the time I stopped putting in flower beds, I had more flowers than I knew what to do with. They had become a problem.

Todd was proud of his soil. "It's the best in the whole valley. Those plants will go crazy."

They did. Within the first year, the roses I'd planted by the weeping cherry were taller than my head. So were the Shasta daisies and the Echinacea. After their root shock, the maples started putting out new growth. Suddenly there were trees and patches of shade, where before there had been hot, glaring sun. Now I had a thousand feet of perennial beds to maintain. It was out of control.

In the meantime, of course, there was still the issue of the sheep. One day, when I had just finished planting a new section of perennials, I stood to get the hose. It was mid-May and already warm. Because I had a lunch date that afternoon, I wore my favorite blue dress and earrings. Rinsing the dirt from my hands, I waved them dry and smoothed my hair into a ponytail. The sheep had finally been sequestered in a pasture by the barn. They didn't like it, but it was them or me. I thought I was winning.

I glanced at my phone. Almost noon. Shoot. I was late. I turned to find my sweater and froze in disbelief. There was Tuffy, the lead sheep, heading up the hill straight for my flower beds. Her mad little eyes looked right at me. She knew exactly what she was doing. I scrambled for my phone.

"Todd!"

"Yeah, what's up, sweetie?" I could hear the whine of saws in the background.

"The sheep!"

"What about them?"

"They're out!" I didn't realize this was a common occurrence. That's why Todd abandoned the fences years ago. Tuffy was an escape artist.

Silence.

"Well, get some grain and put them back in."

I didn't know the first thing about sheep. Back on my family farm, we'd had horses and chickens. The sheep scared me. They ran in a tight pack, all lumped together. They didn't move or veer off course until you were right in front of them.

I ran down to the barn. Out of grain. I speed-dialed Todd's number.

"There's a bag of chips in the kitchen. Just shake it above your head. Yell, *hup, hup*! They'll come."

"A bag of chips?" I was almost crying. I could see Tuffy already nibbling one of the Shasta daisies I'd just planted.

"Yeah, trust me. It'll work."

I found the chips and cautiously approached the sheep. The ram snorted loudly and lowered his head.

Crinkling the bag, I waved it above my head. "Hup!" I shook the bag. "Hup! Hup!"

The sheep looked up. Their eyes glinted. Their noses twitched. Suddenly, they galloped straight at me. Brandishing the bag above my head, I sprinted for the barn. "Hup!" I yelled, "Hup!"

The herd followed like a wave of water, flowing just at my heels. I was sure they were going to attack. I imagined their hard hooves digging into my skin. I ducked into their corral. "Hup!"

Now what? They crowded around, butting my legs and putting their hot little noses against my skirt. Desperately, I ripped open the bag of chips and poured the contents on the ground. They put their heads down, devouring the chips. I dropped the empty bag and slipped out of the corral. Shutting the gate, I sighed.

Dust covered my legs and sandals. Sweat ran down the back of my neck. Now I was really late for my luncheon. Taking a deep breath, I started up the hill toward the house. I was almost to the yard when I heard hooves pattering behind me.

No. It couldn't be. There was Tuffy leading the herd.

This time I grabbed all the chips I could find. Barbeque. Organic blue corn. Organic white corn. I waved the bags above my head, screaming "Hup!" The sheep followed me into the corral, where I flung chips everywhere. When their heads went down for the chips, I found the hole next to the gate and shoved a piece of plywood across it.

I called Todd. We weren't married yet. This was one of our first conflicts. My voice quavered. "Todd, you need to come home, now. And the sheep… they need a real fence."

◆◆◆◆

In retrospect, I'm surprised that Todd tolerated my flower planting and obsession over fences as well as he did. The day after we got back from Hawai'i, where he had proposed at the hot springs, he started remodeling the house.

"Hi, sweetie," he texted me at work. "Can you pick out some tile at Home Depot today? Whatever you like." And then, as an afterthought, "Maybe kind of simple." After my extravagance with flowers, maybe he thought I'd pick out something wildly exotic. I chose a slate gray for the bathroom floor and a white for the handwashing sink.

The bathroom took a month, then we tackled the exterior. We started with the trim. On my days off I'd help sand, grind, prime, and paint. We went through twelve gallons of Dark Walnut Semigloss. We painted for weeks, every night after work, until the sun set and dusk fell.

After the trim was done, we had to pressure spray the whole house and prime it with a thick, pink liquid that looked like Pepto Bismol. After this, the stucco guys came and re-stuccoed the exterior in an earthen brown.

Suddenly, with the red roof tiles and walnut trim, the house looked like a European cottage from a Grimm's fairy tale. I was ecstatic. Tucked between my new trees and flower beds, the place had become a home.

After this, I left for a short-term teaching job in India. It might seem strange to leave your children and fiancé right before your wedding, but I did. What was even more bizarre, we'd set the wedding date for a week after I returned, and the sale of my house up Libby Creek was due to close two days before the wedding. It was utter chaos.

My mother called me on Monday after I returned. "Hi, honey, what are you doing today?"

I was in the garden picking apricots. With a wedding in five days and moving my entire household in three days, what else should I be doing?

In Ladakh, apricots grew everywhere. The villagers sold apricot oil and roasted apricot kernels. Now that I was home, I wanted to make jam from the apricots on my trees. It was the first crop we'd gotten, and it would be my last.

"I'm making jam." I grimaced.

"You're doing what?"

"Jam."

"Julie, do I need to come over?"

"Maybe."

When Mom arrived, she surveyed the living room. Not a box in sight. No packing materials, no stacks of books or clothes. Just twelve pints of apricot jam on the countertop.

"Honey, are you okay?"

I wasn't okay. I was completely overwhelmed. We started with the upstairs and worked our way down. My mother made coffee and helped the girls organize their things. I went to town to pick up the U-Haul.

When I arrived at Todd's house, I could hear NPR playing on the radio. He was in the upstairs office with a floor sander and a face mask. I hadn't seen the house since June. It was transformed. Todd had built bedrooms for each of the girls with matching cubbies in the mudroom for shoes and backpacks. They had their own kitchen, two bathrooms and a loft for two of the girls to share. The upstairs floors were newly finished, and the kitchen demolition was set for next Tuesday.

I walked upstairs and stood in the empty living room. For a moment, everything was quiet. Through the windows, I could see the river, sparkling in the late afternoon sun. Across the field sat the barn with the sheep in their corral. My new flower beds were in full bloom. The grass was green.

Suddenly I remembered a conversation I'd had back in India. I'd met a guy who was visiting the famous Hemes monastery just outside of Leh. He was a Tibetan Buddhist and knew Andrew Harvey, the writer who made Ladakh famous. Now he was asking me about my life.

"Are you here for the summer?"

"Actually, I'm going home to get married next week," I had answered.

He studied my face. Although he was from New York, he seemed to have clairvoyant powers. He had that mystical air of people who spend months meditating in a cave, and as it turned out, he had. I wanted to ask him if it would all work out. I wanted a blessing or some sign that I was doing the right thing. But I couldn't make myself ask.

He chuckled. "Congratulations."

"I have two daughters. He has three."

He smiled. "It will be what it is."

Now, standing in the living room of my new house, I thought about that. I didn't know then how hard it would be to combine families. I didn't know that our teenage daughters would fragment and drift apart. I didn't know the stress of it would give Todd cancer. I couldn't see into the future, but looking around, I realized I had come full circle. I had a farm of my own on the river. I remembered how, when we first moved to the farm in Carlton when I was twelve, I wanted to buy all the land and live there forever.

I learned something during the four years of flower planting. I suppose that I also learned this up Libby Creek too, but it impressed me even more at the farm. When you work for something, you learn to love it. All those hours spent weeding, trimming, dead-heading, moving rock—they had a curious effect on me. The yard that I had once rued became a shining jewel of satisfaction. Now, I wandered around in the early mornings, inspecting each new bloom, each new green shoot of growth.

Over the next few years, we would continue to work on the house. We would put in a courtyard with an arbor, a fountain, and grapes. We would put in an outdoor fireplace and more gardens with steppingstones and a Hawthorn tree and wisteria. It would take more work than I ever imagined, but I would grow to love it. In the process, our love for each other would grow deeper. Out of conflict, imperfection, and snarky teenagers would grow the kind of marriage I'd always wanted. The great love of my life, a second time around.

Moving to the Next Best Place

I have a thing for carpenters. I've married two of them in the Methow Valley.

In a small town this can create quite a stir—but I like good, honest work. I like construction sites, the hot sun, the sweet scents of freshly cut wood and leather tool belts. I like men who know how to do things, who can fix stuff. I love the way their trucks smell, and, if I'm honest, I like what construction work does to their bodies. Twenty-five years of lifting, climbing ladders, and balancing on scaffolding is great for the post-forty physique.

A couple of weeks ago, I stopped by the job site with lattes and muffins for the guys. As I climbed out of the car, I heard NPR playing on the radio. A jar of homemade kombucha sat in the shade, along with a box of tomatoes from someone's garden. Picking my way around stacks of lumber and table saws, I waved at Todd, balanced precariously on some scaffolding.

"Hi!" I held up the tray of lattes.

He grinned and turned to make his way down.

"Hey, there." Jason, the owner of the construction company, walked up behind me, shading his cell phone with his hand. "How's it going?"

"Good." I glanced at the house. I hadn't seen this home yet but had heard in detail about the incessant wind, the lack of water, and the steep driveway—all things that drive guys crazy when building a house.

The house itself was perched on the edge of a steep hill overlooking the valley, with views toward Highway 20 and Mazama. It had a simple design, but even with my untrained eyes, I could tell it was expensive. "A million-dollar shed," as the guys referred to it.

"Like the soffit?" Jason laughed.

The soffit had been a source of contention. The homeowner had changed his mind several times, and the crew ended up ripping out the original wood and replacing it with vertical grain.

"Looks good to me."

"Tell him his friends will love it," Todd winked as I handed him a coffee.

"I just did." Jason finished his text to the homeowner.

Most of the guys here did, in fact, go to college. They discuss politics and world events while they eat their gluten-free lunches and pass around produce from their gardens. Last week, Todd brought home elderberry syrup one of the guys had made. Another carpenter shared his recipe for apple butter. Clearly, these are not your run-of-the-mill construction types.

◆ ◆ ◆ ◆

Sadly, these carpenters are dying out. You might say they're an endangered species in the Methow. They're disappearing because working people, like everyone I used to know, are getting priced out. The Methow has always been a hard place to make a living. People don't move here for the job opportunities. Back in the '60s, before Highway 20 went in, kids who grew up here left and never came back.

During the '70s when Aspen Ski Corporation bought development rights on Lucky Jim Bluff in Mazama, people started moving in. Some were ski bums from Aspen, looking for the next boom. But some were hippie kids in search of lifestyle and community. They clashed with the locals who couldn't see how they could make an honest living. A lot of them had trust funds, but their lifestyle was modest. They bought land, built houses, and farmed for a while. Eventually they had kids and joined the school board, the PTA, and other community organizations. They made friends and formed a web of relationships that would see them through their kids' graduation parties, grandkids, fire seasons, divorces, and everything else that life threw at them. The '70s transplants formed a cohort of people that shaped the Methow for the next thirty years. Their values were grounded in preservation, the land, and simple living.

A similar wave of transplants arrived in the late '90s. This was my cohort. Like the '70s kids, they believed in organic gardening and simple living. They had college degrees from good schools. Some had trust funds. A few had sold Internet companies and built lavish houses, but this was the anomaly, not the norm.

Back then you could buy a starter home for a couple hundred thousand or a piece of property for $50,000. You could do odd jobs or start a business. Some couples started breweries. Some worked for the U.S. Forest Service, but most of the men drifted into construction because you could make more money building houses than doing just about anything else in the Methow.

◆◆◆◆

"Lattes, what a treat!"

I handed a cup to Ben, one of Todd's workmates.

He took a sip. "Thanks."

Ben moved here a few years ago from Leavenworth. "You can't live there anymore," he said. "It's completely outpriced. There's nothing in town. You have to live in Wenatchee or Cashmere and commute."

With the home construction at more than $300 a square foot, and on Todd's wages at $27 an hour, the average worker would have to work ninety-two hours a week—around nineteen hours a day—to afford a home.

Ben shook his head. "Man, that's gonna be one hell of a snowplow."

The four of us turned to contemplate the driveway—a 60-degree slope cut into the side of the hill, exposed to a dizzying drop-off. Homesteaders never built their homes on hills. They built them in the valleys, near creeks. It wasn't until the mid-1990s that houses began popping up on ridgelines and mountain tops. Today people want a view, and they want a house to go with it.

◆◆◆◆

Shackitecture is the term for these pieces of art. It was first applied to local architect Doug Potter's designs from the 1970s. Eventually, it caught the attention of trend-setting Seattle architects like Ray and Mary Johnston, Stefan Hampden, and Tom Lenchek, who started building homes for themselves in the Methow. Their houses quickly gained popularity. Today, nearly all the homes in the Methow are designed in the Methow Modern or Methow Shed style—named after their inspiration from existing barns and sheds and the prevalence of recycled lumber, metal siding, and shed roofs. The modernist movement has acquired so much notoriety it was featured in a lead article in the *Wall Street Journal* last year. As author Nancy Keates put it, "People who come to ski, hike, and mountain bike tend to want a structure that is small, with visual nods to the barns and sheds that already exist there."

The houses, when finished, reflect a dizzying array of mountain views, twenty-foot custom glass doors, metal siding, exposed beams, minimalist bedding, and hand-blown glass fixtures. They're featured every year in *Methow Home*, a *Methow Valley News* supplement, with glowing descriptions like *creative*, *one-of-a-kind*, or a *modern paradise with sweeping views of pristine wilderness*. "I feel like we inspired people," said one homeowner who built a modern home with steel columns and a warped shed roof that neighbors initially complained about. Maybe inspiration is the new draw.

Today's migrants are different from the past two generations. They're tech people. They're savvy. Sophisticated. A few have Learjets and housecleaners. They build separate homes for their gear, which changes according to the season. They have road bikes, mountain bikes, touring bikes, fat bikes, and cross bikes. They have classic skis, skate skis, and alpine skis. They have white-water kayaks, river kayaks, and paddle boards. They have climbing gear as well as running gear (there is such a thing), snowshoes, water bladders, water filters, and even saltwater gear for when they go back to Seattle. They work remotely for Microsoft, Amazon, Google, and other tech companies.

And they like nice houses. Over the years of being married to carpenters, I have visited dozens, maybe hundreds, of new homes and listened to the homeowner talk about the building process with an almost religious reverence. They describe the time spent visiting the Methow, skiing, hiking, recreating. The inspiration to start looking for property, the long search, the serendipitous visit from a friend who also owns property here, and the evening they found "their spot." And then construction—the design, the materials, the indoor stucco, the careful contemplation of products. No Home Depot countertop samples, paint chips, or laminate floor products grace these homes. They describe the local cabinet maker (a friend of mine) who comes to measure the space over a glass of wine, where conversation drifts from wood choices to recent trips abroad and back again, while the homeowner gets a feel for the artisan. Not just anyone works on these homes, and it's important to know who's building your custom wine wall.

◆◆◆◆

The sun blazed down on my head. It was already blistering hot. Todd and Ben handed me their cups and hurried back to work.

Picking my way around piles of wood scraps and other construction materials, I gazed out over the valley floor. From here, I could see the river, silently winding its way toward the Columbia. I could see the East County Road where we lived, and if I looked hard enough, I could make out our section of river, the green fields, and the red tiled roof of our own little house in the Methow.

What was it about these homes that bothered me? Carving out one's own personal art project on the side of hill was nothing new, nor was the sense of pride, of beauty, of aesthetics. People first started stuccoing the walls of their Neolithic villages 12,000 years ago, and I was glad these houses were tasteful. They blended in with the surroundings. They weren't manufactured homes.

But I couldn't shake the sense that the Methow was being colonized all over again. The new generation building homes and moving in saw the landscape differently. They saw "wilderness" while I saw a hillside dotted with homes where years ago there was nothing but sagebrush and spring beauties. They saw "wildlife" while I saw over-populated herds of whitetail deer, which were never native here.

The homeowner saw the expansive view, while the guys building this million-dollar home saw how much the driveway would cost to keep plowed in the winter.

Another aspect that troubled me was their lack of curiosity about what came before them. While many tourist destinations play on the past (the Old West theme of Winthrop, as one example), second homes in the Methow have nothing to do with the past. Homeowners talk about "discovering" the Methow as though it were brand new.

Years ago, I wrote my Master's thesis on this topic. I hypothesized that part of the second home appeal was a sense of nostalgia, that people wanted to go back to some golden time when landscapes were "pure" and unadulterated by development and mechanization. They wanted their own "piece of paradise," I wrote, based on a mythic past of living at one with nature.

I no longer think this is the case. The new amenity migrant is not interested in the Old West theme, nor do they care about the Methow's convoluted history or the American Indian groups who lived here before any of us—and who still live an hour away today.

I teach on the border of the Colville Confederated Tribes Indian Reservation at a branch campus of Wenatchee Valley College. My students are a mixture of Colville members, Latin American immigrants, and old white ranchers' kids. They drive from all over eastern Washington—Moses Lake, Brewster, Bridgeport, Oroville, and Tonasket—but not the Methow. The Methow is too good for Wenatchee Valley. But I love teaching here. My students understand anthropology in ways I never will.

This week we're studying subsistence patterns. They understand subsistence because they live it. The Latinx kids work in the orchards on weekends and after school. The Colville kids grew up hunting and fishing with their grandparents. Yesterday, I showed a film on traditional farming and food sharing in Hawai'i, where I did fieldwork several years ago.

I was always under the impression that the Hawai'ian community in which I have lived and written about was similar to the Methow. Both had small, rural populations, and both were dependent on tourism. But watching the film again I was struck by the difference between the Methow and Hawai'i. The old people in the film told stories about raising taro, hunting in the mountains with dogs, gathering opihi, and fishing. Every reference they made had to do with their parents or an auntie, an uncle, a grandmother. The past was kept alive in the ongoing stories that spontaneously bubbled up when two people from the same family got together. Their culture was based not only on the land, but on the family ties that kept them together.

It struck me that this is where the land-based culture of the Methow differs so drastically from traditional land-based economies. Land-based economies are family-based economies. Recreation economies are based on the individual and on what you can do for leisure, for pleasure. Mountain biking, hiking, trail-running, and Nordic skiing are activities for people with time and money. And not having old people or children dragging behind helps.

Perhaps the mythic past of farming or getting back to the land was a feature of the 1990s immigration, but that's no longer the case. Most remote workers are not looking to farm organically or raise children. They are not dependent on extended families. Many of them do not have children. Most are retired early or looking to retire. Their tie to the land is strictly recreational, not utilitarian. They learn to Nordic and skate ski. They buy all the newest gear. They might frame a map of the wilderness areas to hang on their wall, but it functions as much for decoration as for use.

Like the Modern Methow homes themselves, second homes look to the future. The modern aesthetic, the minimalist couches and furnishings, the views of big expanses—all point to a future of solitude, of careful socializing with peers and friends, of recreation, and of part-time online work. There are few gardens or hobbies to tie one to the land here. No chickens or cats or kids.

This future world is one without messy family ties, sanitized by wealth, glamorized by mountain views, and curiously devoid of complication.

◆◆◆◆

Several years ago, I was invited to an open house at one of the Methow Modern homes that Ken and his crew had recently finished. The house sat at the edge of a field, overlooking the river and, beyond that, the dark, craggy walls of Lucky Jim Bluff. When I arrived, swanky music played from overhead speakers.

A dozen guests plus a handful of construction workers milled around, munching on hors d'oeuvres and drinking wine. The homeowner's wife, Sue, handed me a glass of wine.

"Welcome."

"Thank you." I glanced around. "Beautiful home."

"Do you want to see the rest?"

"Sure."

Sue walked me through the house, pointing out design details she had chosen—a custom bunkbed for the grandchildren, an inset library for the sitting room. The house had floor-to-ceiling windows on one side, a shed roof, and minimalist furnishings and décor. It felt clean and empty. I thought about my house with the girls' artwork taped to the refrigerator and my collection of masks, vases, and artifacts from my travels. Suddenly, my house seemed kitschy and cluttered.

"It's very clean. I mean, it's beautiful." My cheeks flushed. "Gorgeous design."

Sue laughed. "Well, we don't live here fulltime. Come on, I'll show you the kitchen."

In the kitchen, a stainless-steel wonder of sinks, countertops, and refrigerators, Sue's friend and private chef from Los Angeles was preparing a late lunch of carpaccio and dilled potatoes. "Meet Liam!" Sue called over the clatter of dishes.

Liam waved and continued slicing the red salmon. "Hope you're hungry!"

I found some more wine and slipped into conversation with a couple who had just returned from Myanmar.

"We wanted to take the kids before it's totally destroyed. The temples and the statuary alone—my God. It was amazing," the woman said, shaking her head. "I think next year we might try Borneo. What do you think, honey?"

Over dinner, I sat next to Liam, who asked me about my fieldwork in Hawaii. As it turned out, he had a home on the Big Island as well. "You wouldn't know the place. It's new and very small."

"Try me." I took a bite of salmon with yogurt sauce. "This is excellent by the way."

Liam waved away my compliment. "I couldn't find the fish I wanted. Our home is in Kohanaiki. Just north of Kona."

I did know Kohanaiki. The luxury homes in Kohanaiki ranged from four to twenty million dollars each. "Yeah, I visited some friends there once. It's very nice."

At that point, Sue directed a question down the table to me. "Julie, tell us about your teaching." She paused to explain. "Julie's an anthropologist. She teaches at a local college."

I took a deep breath.

I thought about my students. This quarter I had Maurice, who lived with his dad near Tonasket. He was saving money to buy property by raising pit bulls and holding dog fights in his basement. It was illegal but great money. I just hoped he'd learn his lesson before the police picked him up again. Then there was the brother-sister pair, who took all the same classes so they could share textbooks. They walked to school because they didn't have a car. They were Colville and proud of their grandparents, who raised them on fishing and hunting stories from the old days. How could I explain how smart these kids were? How tenacious? And yet, most of them would never finish their AA degrees. Most of them would have their laptop stolen, their car broken into. They might get a DUI over the weekend or get pregnant before the year was out. They might become homeless because their uncle kicked them out, and on and on. Sitting at the table with music in the background and expensive wine in my glass, I stumbled.

"Well, it's a different world."

I launched into a story about taking my sociology students to the county jail for our section on deviance. I described how half the class didn't show up because they'd just gotten out of jail or they had a relative there. I made it hysterically funny. I painted myself as the bumbling teacher who didn't have a clue, and everyone laughed. But as I spoke, my stomach sank. I was doing my students a disservice. Their lives weren't funny, and the poverty they lived with every day wasn't either.

Maybe that's what really bothers me about Methow Modern homes. It's the increasing divide between the haves and the have-nots. Between the people who can obsess over the grain on their soffit, and the kids who walk to school because they don't have a car. It's not just in Omak. It's here, too. But the amenity migrant who moves to the Methow today doesn't see poverty. They see the views and the 1,023 new homes that look like theirs. They feel like they belong because everyone they meet looks like them, talks like them, and believes like them. It's a parallel world, with two classes who will never meet. Just the people like me and the carpenters who dance back and forth between both.

◆◆◆◆

Back at the job site, I blew Todd a kiss and turned to leave. He waved and texted me a heart emoji. As I drove away, I saw another job site across the driveway where a crew of guys were digging out a new foundation. How long will it be before workers start driving from Omak and Okanogan to build these houses? Will it be one year or five? When I was a kid I used to worry about development. I thought that when I was grown, the Methow would look like Wenatchee or Burlington. I cried when I thought of stop lights and ugly industrial buildings.

We're lucky that change has been slow. The '70s migrants helped preserve the Methow with years of coalitions, lawsuits, and fighting with the county over zoning laws. Without them, who knows? Maybe the Methow would look like Wenatchee.

The other alternative isn't great either. Without gentrification, rural places slip deeper into poverty. Take Omak or Okanogan, for example. Drive through either town today and see a burnt-out landscape of empty buildings and boarded-up businesses.

Back in the '80s when my family lived in Bridgeport, Okanogan was the county seat, and Omak was a thriving business community with middle-class families and strong ties throughout the region. Today, over a quarter of the population lives below the federal poverty level, and on the reservation unemployment runs between 20 and 30 percent. Meth, heroin, and homelessness are chronic problems. Last year, the college had to hire a security guard to keep homeless people from wandering into classrooms. Over the last three decades, while the Methow has become an elite enclave, the rest of the county has been left behind.

Driving home on the back road, I rolled my windows down and breathed in the scent of freshly cut hay. *For now*, I thought, *I can afford to live here.* I hope my daughters will be able to as well.

The Wild

It's official. I have decided not to hike on Washington Pass.

If you read this, or by the time you read this, it won't matter that I'm using real place names because Washington Pass (i.e. Highway 20, Gateway to the North Cascades) has been "discovered." If you take a drive today from Seattle and head over Highway 20, you'll take your place in line with a thousand motorhomes, camper vans, and Harley Davidson motorcyclists, and a million SUVs, Sprinter vans, Priuses, and Subarus with bikes and Thules strapped to their rooftops.

You'll be amazed by the scenery. It is spectacular. You'll stop at the Washington Pass Overlook or somewhere along the top near the Liberty Bell spires and get out of your car. You'll breathe in the cool mountain air. The peaks, exploding around you, will glow in the afternoon light. You'll think you've found paradise. And you have… along with a million other people.

It may seem strange, but although I grew up here I never hiked on Washington Pass until I was an adult. Actually, until I had small children.

Growing up, my dad always grumbled about Washington Pass. "Too many people," he'd say, shaking his head. He refused to set foot on Highway 20 past Mazama. So, having never been there, except for driving over the pass to Seattle, I was oblivious to the ease and bounty of Washington Pass. Instead of a six-mile slog and a 4,000-foot climb to see a glimpse of white peaks or an alpine flower, you get out of your car and you're already there: views of alpine meadows, glacier lilies, and snowfields right from the highway.

Which is part of the problem.

The first time I went for a hike on the pass, we had just moved back from New Zealand. Mia and Annika were two and five respectively, and I was determined to fill our summer with enriching hikes and educational forays into the woods. I brought along our plant identification guide, journals to document our nature experience, and baggies of Cheerios and raisins. As it turned out, the Cheerios and raisins spilled before we left the trailhead, and Mia dumped her water in the first half mile. By the time we made it to Cutthroat Lake, the girls were tired, hungry, and thirsty.

"This isn't lunch, Mommy!" Annika wailed when she looked in her pack.

But I was hooked. As a solo mother with two kids, I could do this.

Washington Pass became our playground. We hiked every trail so many times we got to know them by heart. I was reading *Last Child in the Woods* that summer, which quieted my inclination to gripe about all the people. A firm believer in nature-deficit disorder, I was determined to get my kids into nature, and the fact that a hundred thousand other people were doing the same thing was… well, I tolerated it.

The truth was, we lived up Libby Creek and had a little more nature than we could handle. That summer a cougar ate our beloved cat while we screamed hysterically from the living room window. Bears routinely rambled through the property, and the previous week, a bobcat had surprised me on our porch at 7 AM. While I loved our property, I was more worried about walking down to the pond than hiking eight miles on Washington Pass. We were surrounded by nature so deep and wild, I worried about letting the girls play in the yard.

So Washington Pass became one of our sacred summer routines. Once a week we'd grab our packs and a favorite book and head to Mazama. I got better at lunches. Once we started stopping at the Mazama Store, we never looked back. Instead of cheese cubes and raisins, we stocked up on croissants and Danishes. I even got something called the Figgy Piggy, a homemade Danish filled with fig jam and bacon bits. Excellent with a double-tall Americano. I never shirked on goods from the Mazama Store. They became my primary bargaining tool to get the girls to go with me. They could pick out whatever they wanted. Black velvet, cream cheese cupcake? Sure. A five-dollar slice of olive oil cake? You bet. Over the years we came to associate hikes on Washington Pass with the best baked goods you can buy east of the Cascades. Every hike was a success.

Until the summer of 2019, when the girls and I decided to hike to Blue Lake. Of all the hikes on the pass, this had been my last choice, simply because it was the most popular. Everyone hiked Blue Lake. My friends routinely trail-ran it before spinning class at the gym. Their kids were running it before they hit fifth grade. It was obnoxious, so we stayed away. When I finally hiked it with the girls, I realized why it was far and away the most popular trail on Highway 20. It's so easy, it's cheap. In less than three miles you get the best alpine views and a crystal-clear glacial lake bordered by the backside of the Liberty Bell spires, which are arguably some of the most awesome rock configurations on the planet. So, yes. Blue Lake is cool. It is also popular. And a hike that you can do with children. Be forewarned.

When we got to the trailhead, there were fifty-three cars in the parking lot. We counted them. There were another forty-three vehicles parked along the highway. I counted those, too, because I was mad and had already decided to call the Park Service to complain. My attitude didn't bode well for our afternoon, but we persevered. We had vanilla-almond Danishes in our backpack. It couldn't be too bad.

"Okay, girls. Let's just do this. It'll be fun."

Annika's eyebrows curved down dangerously. Her bottom lip protruded into its most fierce pout. Her eyes glared. She hated people on trails. She strapped on her running shoes and silently took off. So much for mother-daughter bonding.

I sighed and glanced at Mia, who flipped our dog Pepper's leash lethargically. Already I could see the discontent brewing on her forehead.

"Let's go. Quick, before that family gets out of their car." I turned away and hurried up the trail. The only way to hike with Mia was to ignore the grumbling.

We hustled through the woods. Old-growth cedars and delicate green ferns lined the trail. Woodpeckers drilled in the canopy, and camp robbers called above our heads. Sunlight filtered through the trees, landing in patches of yellow along the forest floor.

Behind us, a toddler's wail pierced the air. Adult voices shouted. A dog barked. I glanced back. Mia was trailing behind, messing with Pepper. A half-Papillon, half-Chihuahua mix, Pepper resembled a hairy fruit bat the size of a cat.

Pepper was not in the mood to hike, either. She kept diving off the trail to sniff various roots and needle-covered holes.

"Pick it up, Mia," I snapped. "Faster."

Mia gave me a withering look and pushed past. I watched as her long, brown legs disappeared up the trail, her blond ponytail bouncing with rage. Anger was one of her few motivators.

Alone, I tried to speed walk. It was hot. Sweat cooled the back of my neck. I laced my fingers behind my pack to still its walloping as I walked. I was carrying all the water, the plant guide, Mia's paint set, and Annika's book. As I settled into a steady pace, I passed the first group of people coming down.

"Hello," I intoned politely, stepping to the side.

The couple, a guy in his early thirties and a girl in her twenties, brushed by without looking up. Earbuds trailed from their ears. I realized they couldn't hear me. I don't think they saw me, either.

I heard the next group before I saw them. A pack of families clustered together with half a dozen kids, trekking poles, packs, and a pair of black Labrador retrievers. The women were talking about running Green Lake, while the men discussed the pros and cons of a new software they were using at work. I knew this because their conversation took place over a quarter mile of trail, and their voices floated through the forest like a megaphone. Music blared from their kids' iPods. By the time I stepped aside and gave them a nod, I felt like I knew them on a first-name basis. Having heard about Molly's running shoes for the last five minutes, I almost suggested she get a new pair.

Next came a group of elderly hikers. They wore sunhats with flaps covering their ears and enormous smiles. "Hello!" They waved cheerfully.

"Hello." Stepping aside, I smelled sunscreen and Old Spice aftershave. I hoped I smelled as good. I was starting to sweat in earnest as I picked up my pace to an awkward jog. No matter how fast I hurried, I couldn't catch up with Annika or Mia. They must be really mad.

By the time I broke out into the meadows below the lake, the sun blazed down in a sweltering 90-plus degrees. Why hadn't I brought my swimsuit? We usually found a private spot and jumped in in our underwear, but I could tell that wasn't going to happen today.

Huffing up the last incline, I jerked to a halt. Before me stood a shaggy white mountain goat. He was young, probably an adolescent. His sides heaved wildly. His eyes rolled. Just beyond the goat crouched a father and son, taking pictures.

"Here, Tyler!" The dad maneuvered his way closer to the goat. "Let's get a selfie."

Trapped between me and the father-son duo, the goat paused. Close on my heels, a German couple who had been gaining on me for the past mile now pushed past, cameras whirring. They exclaimed eagerly, stretching out their hands to pet the goat.

The goat stamped his feet and snorted.

"I wouldn't do that," I said.

Eyes rolling, the goat shifted his feet. Slowly, I tried to back away, as another family hurried up behind me.

"A goat!" one of the kids screamed.

"Wow, that's so cool," the parents yelled. "Get a picture, Hannah!"

The goat turned to bolt, but surrounded by a dozen people he had nowhere to go. He lowered his head and turned toward one of the dogs, who was barking furiously.

I shook my head. I couldn't watch. Fuming, I darted into the trees and made my way around the crowd and the goat to find the girls.

The girls had fled past the picnic site, packed with people, to the farthest point down the lake.

"Did you see that, Mom?" Annika's face was flushed. "That poor goat! He didn't know what to do."

Mia clutched Pepper, tears rolling down her cheeks. "It wasn't his fault. Those people should have left him alone."

Shrugging off my pack, I collapsed onto a rock. "I know, girls. I know." I didn't know what to say. I was trembling, too. There must have been close to fifty people back there. The goat was confused. I shook my head.

"Why don't people know to leave animals alone?" Mia stomped her foot. "People are so stupid!"

Annika stood, poised to run back for a fight. "Mom, we should do something."

I sighed. From across the lake we heard Beyonce blaring from bad speakers. Someone was playing their iPod for all of us to hear.

◆ ◆ ◆ ◆

The North Cascades National Park was created in 1968, shortly after Congress passed the Wilderness Act of 1964. That same year saw the establishment of the half-million-acre Pasayten Wilderness, and ten years later, the Stephen Matther and Lake Chelan Sawtooth Wilderness areas. The combined area of National Forest, National Park, State, and designated wilderness lands means the Methow is surrounded by 3.6 million acres of public land. While this seems like a lot of space, it's a tiny fraction of the area taken up by urban centers along Puget Sound.

Having a PhD in tourism and anthropology, I've spent most of my life studying the impacts of tourism in remote areas. I've studied tourism in the Himalayas and the Mount Everest region, Ladakh, New Zealand, and Hawai'i. Maybe I study human impact because it helps me cope with the fact that by 2050 there will be more than 15 billion people on the planet. Intellectually, I know we must share our wild spaces with other people. I know that, in order to preserve natural habitat, people must care about the wild. But sitting there at Blue Lake, my thoughts echoed Mia's.

"Why are people so stupid?"

I don't think people mean to be obtuse. We're animals, following the lead of those around us. If fifteen people start taking selfies with a mountain goat, why not? What's wrong with letting your kids play music at a high mountain lake?

When I related this story to a coworker a few weeks later, she said, "Most of those kids don't get to be outside. Maybe they're just having fun and letting off steam."

I thought about this for a long time, and after months of pondering, my only response was: *Because it's wrong.*

My father was an avid outdoorsman. He grew up on a mink farm in Oregon and moved to Washington to escape what he considered "the mess" of Portland. My mother's roots were even more rural, having spent her childhood on a dairy farm in Wisconsin. She attended a one-room schoolhouse with her sister before they moved West. I don't think my parents ever told me not to yell in the woods. It was just something you would never do. When we got outside, we whispered. When we hiked, we didn't talk because we were listening. There was a lot to hear outside. Wind in the trees. The crack of a branch. Footsteps. Birds calling. My dad took me hunting every fall. We learned to be quiet. When you sit on a ridgetop before the sun rises, there's a certain hush to the land. Everything feels like it's holding its breath, waiting. Even the birds who started singing hours ago fall quiet at the exact moment the sun slips over the horizon. You only know this because you're not talking. You're being still.

Being still in nature gives you a sense of your place in the world. Listening to the wind, a creek, the ocean, or birds in the canopy, you feel yourself becoming less significant. The worries and narratives in your head quiet down. The planet is bigger than you. The whole magnificent world is living, breathing, and dying all around you.

Experiencing nature as part of the animal kingdom is what we've been doing for most of our six million years of evolution—until about October 3, 2001, when the first iPod came out. Since then, kids have been plugged into devices as though their lives depended on it. I told my daughters when they were little that screens would rot their brains. Literally. They believed me. If they went to a friend's house and had to watch a movie, Annika would come home crying because her brain had rotted that day.

I eased up over the years. My daughters are custodians of their own minds. Lately Mia spends most of her days on TikTok, but I cling to the hope that all those afternoons in the woods whispering and listening will one day flower into a sense of her place in nature.

◆◆◆◆

Which brings me back to Blue Lake. The girls and I sat for a couple hours, listening to screams and the splash of bodies hitting the water. We munched unhappily on our pastries. Mia did a watercolor sketch of the lake. We tried not to think about the confused goat and all the people who seemed hellbent on destroying our afternoon with their presence. When we finally gathered our things and started back around the lake, I was sure the goat would be gone. I was hoping the people might be, too.

As we pushed our way through the shrubby spruce trees, we stopped short. The goat stood poised in front of a crowd of people. This time, his nostrils flared and spittle flew from his panting mouth. His head swayed drunkenly from side to side. I wondered if he was suffering heat stroke or a panic attack. He was totally freaked out.

The crowd of hikers cheered happily. One little girl picked a handful of grass.

"It's okay, sweetie." Her dad pushed her towards the goat. "You can feed him! He's friendly."

The girl walked up to the goat. He stamped his feet and lowered his head. He ran at her a few feet, then stopped.

"Get your kid!" I yelled, automatically reaching out to grab the girl.

The dad looked at me. "Isn't it cool? He's not afraid."

"Actually, it isn't cool." I was trembling. "There's something wrong with a goat who walks up to a crowd of fifty people. Can't you see how confused he is?"

"Oh." The man glanced at his other kids. He lowered his camera. "Emma, maybe don't feed the goat."

He took her hand and pulled her away.

"Girls, come on." I glanced at Annika and Mia. They looked on the edge of tears. "Let's go."

We hurried past the goat and the crowd. People stared as if we were crazy. Didn't we want a selfie with the goat?

◆◆◆◆

Mountain goats are native to the North Cascades. At one time their population totaled over 10,000 but hunting over the last century decimated their numbers. Today, there are fewer than 3,000, a third of which live on the Olympic Peninsula.

Traditionally, mountain goats never lived in the Olympics. They were introduced in the 1920s for hunting. While mineral deposits in the Cascades provide the salt they crave, there are no such deposits in the Olympics. Over time, the peninsula goat population has lost its fear of humans and grown aggressive.

They're attracted to salt from human sweat and urine. After several attacks on dogs and humans, the National Park Service decided to relocate part of the goat population. Since 2018, 275 goats have been relocated, most of them to our corner of the North Cascades.

When I called the Park Service later that afternoon, the ranger I spoke with confirmed that, indeed, they had just relocated seven goats near Blue Lake.

"Was it a young male?" she asked.

"I think so. He looked about a year old."

"I'm not surprised. He just arrived last week. I heard he was charging dogs up there."

I didn't fault the goat, but rather a public uninformed about how to treat wild animals. "I think you need signs or something telling people to stay clear of animals," I said. "And maybe close the parking lot once it's full. There were forty-three cars along the highway. It's a liability."

"I know." The ranger sighed. "We don't have the funding. It's an absolute mess."

Wild animals who become habituated to humans are always a problem. It's not their fault. It's ours. Todd often tells us the story of when he was working in the Arctic and one of the guys fed the Arctic foxes. One mother fox grew so habituated she stopped hunting and taught her cubs to beg for scraps. One day, when the man reached out to give her a bone, she bit him and ripped his hand to shreds. The guy lost his job, and the fox was killed. Her cubs died because they'd never learned to hunt and be wild.

There are hundreds of stories about humans interacting with wild animals, from toddlers being raised by wolves to people like the grizzly guy who lived with (and was killed by) the bears in Alaska. We humans want to believe we have a connection with wild animals. And we do; but the connection is fragile and depends on us understanding that, in order to survive, animals have to be wild. It took thousands of years to domesticate a few species on the planet. Out of millions of mammals, only fourteen species have been successfully domesticated. They now depend on humans for survival. Once an animal is tamed, it can't go back.

I think about this in a larger sense. Our wild places are being domesticated. We're losing them through people and everything we bring with us—our ignorance, our chatter, our litter. Instead of listening when we're outside, we bring iPods so we can hear music. Maybe we even download a movie so we can watch a screen instead of the night sky. We bring friends so we won't be alone. We bring our phones and cameras to capture every moment so we can share it on Facebook or Instagram to document that we got "out" over the weekend. Sadly, we didn't get out. We didn't get out of ourselves one bit.

I know I'm the last generation who grew up without the Internet. I know my childhood was different than my children's or their children's will be. I know it's clichéd to rue technology when it enables my own lifestyle and my ability to live in a beautiful place where I can work remotely. And I know I'm part of the problem. My presence in the mountains is no better than anyone else's.

But I'd like to think we can do better. I'd like to think that we could train our kids to value solitude and silence, to grow their spirits as well as their minds.

Most indigenous cultures had some kind of coming-of-age ritual, whether a walkabout or a vision quest. Granted, as a mother, the thought freaks me out. But what if we could let go of the illusion of control our technology gives us? What if we left our phones and our iPods behind when we went to the mountains? We can do better at keeping places wild. We can do better at keeping animals wild too.

When we got home from Blue Lake that summer, we sat in our car for a minute. There was silence. I glanced in the rearview mirror. Annika glared out the window. Mia was asleep. One of our summer routines had come to an end. It wasn't so much the end of our day hikes, but the sense that something else had ended. We felt it.

The Methow had lost something. Maybe it was becoming habituated to the selfies and Thules and recreational gear. Like all creatures, once places lose their wild, they never get it back.

Living with Fire

One thing you need to know about living in the Methow is fire. Fire is a big part of our lives. We fear it, we use it, we make money from it, and we live with it—every summer.

Sometimes, residents date the years by the fire season. They'll say, "That was 2001. The Thirty Mile Fire." Or, "2014. Carlton Complex." Over the last twenty years, 50 percent of the Methow River watershed has burned—256,000 acres of mostly public land.

My first fire season was 1994. I was in India, but I imagined it through my mother's handwritten letters that arrived weeks later. She described the smoke, the spotter planes flying overhead, and how everything looked like a sepia photograph for weeks. It sounded like a war zone. Before 1994, it rained in the summer. I used to lean my head out the window before a storm. The air smelled sweet and nutty like grass, pine trees, and rain. Thunderstorms came with rain back then.

After 1994, summers got hotter. Dryer. Rain was scarce.

The next fire season that I remember clearly was 2000. Harts Pass burned that summer. We lived with smoke for weeks, and when I first saw the Meadows Campground after the fire, I burst into tears. It looked like Mount Saint Helens' eruption. A forest of bare, gray matchstick trees. Every shred of vegetation gone—naked ground.

I know fire is good for the forest. I know that fifty years of fire suppression creates thick, unnatural understory that burns hotter and faster and needs cleaning out. In the Methow, we're familiar with fire science. But for those who never saw Harts Pass before 2000, know that it wasn't thick. It wasn't underbrush. It was high-alpine old-growth forest, with green meadows and streams. It was magical. After the fire, it looked, sadly, like a recovering cancer patient. Bald, skinny, almost dead.

The next year was 2001. Thirty Mile. Thirty Mile changed how the U.S. Forest Service fought fire because four firefighters died. I saw the plume from Harts Pass. It was hot—90-plus degrees at 8,000 feet. The air was so dry it felt like I was breathing inside an oven. The plume started as a wisp of smoke. Within hours, it mushroomed into a cloud shape. By the time I got to my car at the trailhead, it looked like pictures I'd seen of Hiroshima. A towering mountain of white puffy clouds, silently spilling into the crystalline sky. You couldn't tear your eyes away. It didn't seem like smoke. It looked surreal, like clouds in a fairy tale, but it kept growing—white puff upon puff. It was beautiful.

Until it fell. When it fell the whole valley filled with smoke as thick as night.

Three of the four firefighters were rookies, kids just out of high school. They'd been mopping up the remains of a fire from someone's campsite. Everyone considered it an easy job. The crew had spread out along the narrow canyon when the fire exploded out of control, jumping the road and cutting off their escape route. Half the crew piled in a truck and drove through the wall of flames. The other half were stuck. They deployed their fire shelters in the middle of the road. Some crew members were afraid a truck might run over them, so they chose the rocky hillside. One guy panicked and jumped in the creek. The survivors said it sounded like a train coming at them. They lay in their shelters and prayed. They worried that the seams of their tents would explode. When it passed, they crawled out. They looked around. They started calling. That's when they realized that four out of their twelve were missing.

Detailed accounts of the Thirty Mile Fire have been published. In the Methow, it went down as the most horrific event that had ever happened here. It made national news and might have gone on to be a feature film, had not one event overshadowed it. Two months later, on the day of the commemoration ceremony for the firefighters who died, two passenger planes flew into the Twin Towers and made history bigger than ours.

◆◆◆◆

After Thirty Mile, I was definitely scared of fire. I knew how quickly it can travel. I knew how disorienting smoke can be. More than anything, I never wanted to get caught in a forest fire.

The summer of 2010 started out idyllic. Ken and I were married and lived up Libby Creek where a wet spring drifted into a hot summer. We had planted an enormous garden. By August it was in full production. Red potatoes, green beans, kale, beets, summer squash, and cucumbers accompanied every meal. Kenny wanted to go backpacking for our anniversary, but I didn't want to leave the girls. We compromised by planning to meet my parents and the kids in Stehekin, at the end of Lake Chelan. Ken and I would hike over and spend the night at Juanita Lake, while they took the boat.

A week before our trip, dry lightning ignited several fires. The valley filled with smoke. Everyone started irrigating heavily.

The fire season had begun.

"I don't think we should go," I said.

"It'll be fine. It's not that close."

"Still…"

I convinced Kenny to call our friend, the manager at the smokejumper base.

"Where are you going?"

"Juanita Lake."

"Yeah, you should be okay. Just don't head north, or you'll run right into it."

We left early the next morning. Fire is confusing in the mountains because you can't see it. The peaks cut off your view. Even if you can see the smoke plume, you can't tell where it's coming from. It could be twenty miles away—or just over the next ridge.

The South Creek trail follows the creek for about eight miles before launching up a steep scramble to Juanita Lake, nestled near the top of the Sawtooth range. As we hiked, gray smoke filtered through the trees, casting the forest in dirty orange and rose light. Flies bit my arms. Mosquitoes whined in my ears.

I hadn't backpacked in years. My pack felt heavy. It dug into my shoulders. Every step was laborious. I hadn't wanted to go. I didn't want to leave the girls, now four and seven. I worried about the fires. I worried about the garden at home. The dog.

Why were we doing this?

At last we hit the incline before the lake. Whoever had cleared this trail must have gotten tired of switchbacks, because suddenly the trail bounded straight up the mountainside. A miserable hour later, we arrived, panting and exhausted, at the lake.

I'm sure Juanita Lake is beautiful in the spring, but the shallow puddle that greeted us in August was disappointing. Stagnant water rippled in the breeze. Wildflower blossoms desiccated in the dry meadows. A handful of fir trees grew on one side, and beyond, a cliff rose sharply into the sky.

I shrugged off my pack and collapsed on a log. Kenny busied himself around the campsite, setting up the tent, arranging the cook stove and food. It was oddly quiet except for a wind that blew from the north. Biting my lip, I studied the ridgeline above the lake. Behind it, you could see a brown plume of smoke. I sniffed. Fresh. Sometimes you can smell the difference in smoke. Close, fresh smoke smells piney, sharp, but far away smoke smells dirty. Like cigarettes. I took a deep breath.

"Ken, I think I'm going to hike up that ridge and see where the fire is."

"Hold on. I'll come, too."

I took a sip from my water bottle. Something landed on my arm. A charred pine needle. When I blew on it, it disintegrated into ash.

"I think we should go now."

"Okay. Let me get my shoes on."

I glanced at my flip flops. I had changed out of my boots, which were hot, dusty, and bruised my toes. Oh, well.

I followed Kenny around the lake. From here, the trail switched back and forth up a rocky scree slope. It was farther than I thought. Picking my way through the rocks, I paused and listened. A breeze cooled my face. It was quiet. Nothing but the wind. Above me, birds flew in a straight line, away to the south. One after another, little birds and bigger birds. That was strange. Suddenly, a bleat broke the stillness. I couldn't place the sound. It came again. Scared, persistent.

Ahead, Kenny had reached the ridgetop. I could see his silhouette against the sky, legs planted far apart, arms at his sides. He stood for a split second before putting his hands to his head, then abruptly, he turned and ran down the trail.

Suddenly, I knew what the sound was. It was the cry of a baby—a goat or maybe a fawn. Something left behind. That's why the birds were flying. They were leaving. A flash of brown scurried near my feet. A ground squirrel. He was moving, too. All the animals were running in the same direction. It reminded me of the scene from *Bambi* in which all the animals flee the fire. They knew what we didn't.

Ken hurried down the trail, breathless. "Now, Julie..." He held out his hand to calm me.

"Jesus Christ." I sucked in my breath. "How close is it?"

"Let's just say I don't think we should stay here tonight."

"How close?"

"No need to panic, but maybe we should pack up."

"Maybe? Maybe we should pack up?"

I think I said many unladylike things. I'm *sure* I did. I remember running in my flip flops and being surprised that I could move that fast. When we got to the campsite, I shoved my feet back into my boots and hoisted my pack.

"Shouldn't we get the tent?" Kenny began to break down the tent poles.

I could hardly answer. Panic tinged my vision. My arms felt tingly. "I'm getting out of here."

Kenny grabbed the food bag and his pack.

We started to run. We ran through the meadow and past the grove of firs. We ran until we hit the pass, where abruptly the trees cleared, and we could see Lake Chelan far below.

And there was the fire.

I didn't know whether to laugh or cry. We were standing a few hundred yards away from a hundred-foot wall of flames. I could hear it. It did sound like a train. It sounded like an engine screaming at you from all directions. You could feel it in the ground, under your feet. The heat blew my hair back. My face felt hot.

"Oh my God." I looked at Kenny, incredulous. "This is it."

"Go. You're faster."

Faster. I'm faster, I thought. *Okay.* I started to move. My legs shook. They felt like rubber. From here, I could see into Stehekin, a tiny village at the end of Lake Chelan. Once I left the pass, I'd be in the trees and I wouldn't see the fire. I wouldn't know where it was. I took one last look at the lake sparkling, 3,000 feet and twelve miles down. Taking a deep breath, I ran.

It didn't occur to me until several miles later that I was wearing my pajama pants. I also wasn't wearing a bra. I had changed into my camp clothes, and now my pants kept slipping down. At least I wouldn't see anyone on the trail. Was the trail even open, or would we get cut off? I managed to fasten my pack around my waist, but I had to hold up my pants as I ran clumsily, panting. I cried a little. Then I cursed Kenny for dragging me out here. Mostly I prayed. I prayed that I would see Annika and Mia again. *Please, God, let me make it. Please, God, let me make it.*

The trail made long sweeping switchbacks down to the lake. Every time the trail switched to the right, we ran toward the fire. *Where is it,* I wondered. *Where is it?* The smoke was so thick I couldn't see anything. I heard trees exploding in the distance and the wind blowing the fire toward us. On one particularly long switchback, I was sure we would get cut off. Below me, smoke poured from the forest, and flames licked up the sides of trees.

"Ken!" I paused and turned. No one. "Kenny!" I screamed. Nothing. I was alone. Shit. Far below, I could see the lake glinting through the trees. Maybe I could find a cliff. I could jump. Would I survive hitting the water from 2,000 feet? Where was Kenny? I screamed until my throat closed. Gone. He was gone. Time to go.

I ran on. At one point, my mind registered something in the trail at my feet. Rattlesnake. I cleared it in one leap and kept going. My mouth tasted metallic. I couldn't swallow. I needed water. After what seemed like forever, I came to a wide creek. Without slowing, I plunged in, the icy current splashing up my legs. I kept going. The trail seemed to level now. I was running through a cleared forest. Ahead, a building. Another building. A Forest Service station. Oh my God. I had made it. I was in Stehekin.

Sobbing with relief, I stumbled up the steps of the ranger station. The door stood open, and from inside I heard soft music playing. People stood around, talking calmly in low voices. They browsed through books, sipping wine and punch. A ranger talk. I had stumbled into one of the evening talks on bears and other wildlife.

I crashed into the room, wet, muddy, and panting. Thirty guests swiveled to stare at me. I tried to say something, but my mouth was dry. My tongue stuck like sandpaper. On the table in the middle of the room sat a bowl of red punch. Never had anything looked so good. I staggered to the punchbowl with my pack dangling from my back. A man standing nearby shoved a cup in my hands. "Here."

I drank.

"Here." He refilled the cup.

"Fire," I gasped when I could speak. "Fire." Didn't they know? Why weren't they evacuated?

The man's face blanched. "Did you come through the fire?"

Suddenly, a ranger appeared at my elbow. "This way, miss." He had snowy hair and a well-trimmed beard. "Right this way."

His grip on my arm told me to be quiet.

"David." He gestured to another ranger, who quickly followed us into a back room. They shut the door.

"Where did you come from?"

"Juanita Lake. The fire was everywhere."

The men frowned.

One of them pulled out a map. "Can you show us exactly where the fire was?"

They didn't know. The smoke was so thick that day in Stehekin that air support couldn't fly. The Park Service had no idea that the fire had crested Sawtooth Ridge and was burning down towards town.

"My husband is gone," I added.

"When did you last see him?"

"I don't know, maybe two hours ago?" I had no sense of time. Outside, it was almost dark.

The men asked me what Kenny looked like and took down his shoe size in a notebook. The guy named David picked up a radio. *Dammit, Kenny,* I thought. *Why didn't you keep up? What happened to you?*

The man with the white hair turned to me. "Can you show us again where the fire was?"

Just then the radio crackled. "Yeah, did you say a guy with a ponytail, beard? We just saw him. He's on his way to the bar. Said he was going to get a Blue Moon."

I laughed through tears. That was definitely Kenny.

The men let me go but made me promise to come back with my husband to show them once more where the fire had crested the ridge.

That night one of the Park Service guys gave us a tent to sleep in since we'd left ours at the lake. Unfortunately, the only restaurant in town was closed, so we had to eat prepackaged salads. Even after traversing twenty miles that day, I couldn't eat. My throat was seared from smoke and screaming. When I closed my eyes, I kept seeing that wall of flames and hearing the roar coming at me. All night I kept watch, dozing in and out of sleep, trying to see through the trees, trying to see the fire.

◆◆◆◆

I wouldn't say I have PTSD, but I will say that fire triggers me. I get jumpy around fire season. Especially after the summers of 2014 and 2015. There are so many fire seasons now, I lose track of them.

In 2020, the fires didn't start until Labor Day, when some sadly deranged people set fires all over the Northwest. As I write this, the air quality index is over 300, hazardous.

Fires are part of climate change. They're also part of humanity. This year most of the fires were started by humans. A spark from a mower. Arson. Someone having a campfire during the burn ban. Someone not putting their fire out. The climate is too dry now. Anything can and will start a fire. I wish people would understand this when they visit the Methow. Their actions affect everyone.

But that night in Stehekin, as I tried to sleep, I wasn't thinking about climate change. I was just glad to be alive. I couldn't wait to see my daughters the next day.

In the morning, we packed our things and tried to hike the four miles from Stehekin to the guest house we planned to rent with my parents. I say "tried," because I could hardly move.

These days I have many friends who run from the Methow to Stehekin. It's a thing here. And I do, too. Last summer, the girls and I ran in from Rainy Pass.

But back in 2010, the year Kenny and I fled the Rainbow Fire, I had never done twenty miles. I was thirty-three years old, finishing my PhD, and mothering. Going for a walk up the road was an accomplishment. Running with a pack almost paralyzed me. My thighs were so sore I practically crawled. To make matters worse, another fire had burned through earlier, and dozens of downed trees blocked the trail. Every hundred yards or so, we had to scramble over a massive tree.

The plan was to meet at the Flick Creek Cabin around noon. We could see a couple of cabins near the lake, but we couldn't tell which one was ours.

"I wish we could ask someone." I brushed a strand of hair from my eyes. It felt gritty. I needed a shower.

"I know." Kenny glanced at the lake. "Maybe I can radio your dad." Stehekin had no phone system or Internet. Kenny had brought a walkie talkie to use with my dad.

Just then I saw a person ahead on the trail. "Hey." I pointed. "Why don't you ask him?"

From behind, it looked like an old man with a hat. He stood in the trail, hunched over.

"Excuse me, sir." Kenny walked up to the man.

The man swiveled his head.

Kenny leaped backwards.

"Whoa!"

It was actually a bear standing on its hind legs. And, as it turned out, it was a female bear with cubs. As we bolted back down the trail, Kenny radioed my dad, who was at the house with the owner.

"Yeah," I heard the owner say. "That bear's been a little aggressive. She's got cubs nearby. I'd better come get you in the boat."

Bears, forest fires, crippled legs. I was starting to lose it.

"Can you see the stone house from where you are?" The man's voice crackled through the radio.

We could. It was right in front of us.

"I'll pick you up there. Meet me down by the dock."

Kenny and I hurried down the driveway. The house looked abandoned. At one time, it must have been beautiful, but now the stone walls crumbled into the ground.

A rock wall lined the pathway down to the dock. The guy on the radio was saying something else, when I heard a sharp rattle near my feet. Inches away coiled one of the largest rattlesnakes I'd ever seen. He was so old and big, he had pointy eyebrows over his eyes. I didn't know this was possible. His diamond-shaped head pulled back to strike. His tongue slithered in and out.

I froze. Rattles echoed on either side.

I'm sure I screamed, but once again, my feet moved of their own accord. I don't know how many snakes were dozing in the sun along the stone wall to the dock, but it felt like a minefield.

The guy in the boat laughed. "Yeah, I was trying to warn you about the snakes. The house was abandoned a while back because the snakes took over. They like those rocks."

◆◆◆◆

A note to any would-be hiker from the Methow to Stehekin: There are lots of bears and lots of snakes. There are also lots of fires.

Fire has changed the way we live in the Methow. Before 2014, everyone wanted their own twenty acres with mountain views and forests. Few people lived in town. A lot of second homes were located up creeks and valleys, far from fire stations and water. After 2014, insurance premiums went up. If you were more than five miles from a fire district, you couldn't get insurance. People started moving to town. There was a period of urban renewal. The town of Twisp invested in sidewalks. People started renovating old homes in Winthrop and building new ones.

A few non-profits got together and formed the Methow Valley Long Term Recovery Group, which is a long title for a group that tries to troubleshoot future catastrophes. One of the outcomes of the MVLTRG was consensus on the need for affordable housing. Some of the people who lost their homes in 2014 didn't have insurance. As is often the case, those who could least afford it lost the most. The Methow Housing Trust, a community land trust, formed in 2017 to offer homeownership with fixed appreciation for low-income residents.

Another result of the fires was the movement to firewise homes by planting fire-resistant plants, thinning trees, or applying metal siding. Firewise became part of the Methow Conservancy's programming and continues to influence architecture and housing styles in the Methow today. Today, most homes are built with minimalist designs that involve lots of metal and shed roofs. Landscaping has become xeriscaping with drought- and fire-resistant plants and lots of gravel.

Affordable housing and the movement to firewise existing homes are certainly admirable. However, the real change is harder to quantify. We can put up metal siding, but it won't slow climate change. We can fight the market and keep a few homes under $300,000, but we can't keep out the world. I think living with fire means living with climate change on a psychic level as well as a physical one. I'll never forget the smoke plumes from the Thirty Mile Fire or the Carlton Complex. Towering mountains of smoke. Eruptions on a scale the world has seldom seen. They were terrifying but beautiful. They were bigger than me, bigger than anyone.

There is a power in the natural world. To me, climate change is the planet's cancer, telling it—telling us—to wake up. When I stood on the pass near Juanita Lake and saw that 100-foot wall of flames coming toward me, I was sure I was going to die in a forest fire. I don't know how close to death I really was, but I felt it. I felt that brush with mortality so close and clear it felt like a kiss.

I don't know how people cope with death. Recently, my husband, Todd, had cancer and watched both his parents die in 2019. Two years later, I almost died from complications during surgery. Death has cast its shadow over us the last few years. I love Todd and my children more every day, but I'm helpless to save them. I can't even save myself. Cancer terrifies me.

So does climate change. I love this planet, but I can't save it. I can't turn the tides of warming, but I live with it anyway. It heightens every summer. It colors every winter. I don't take snow for granted. Rain is better than money in my savings account.

◆◆◆◆

Right now, it's late September and the asters are blooming. Thousands of tiny purple blooms like stars in a sea of green. I'm grateful for seasons. I'm grateful the asters know when to bloom. I'm grateful for clouds in the sky this morning.

I think the fires have made us all kinder. When everything spirals out of control, you can be kind. You can take care of chickens, neighbors, kids. Each other. I don't always remember to be kind, but fire season reminds me to stop. It makes me pause and slow down. Sometimes, I stand in the forest and listen. I listen to the sound of dry leaves and heat shimmering unnaturally through the trees.

I love you, I say. I don't know who I'm saying it to, but I say it anyway. *I love you.*

I love you, world. I love you, trees. I love you.

Study Group

I always wanted to be smart.

My sister was smart. She did Knowledge Bowl in high school, and she scored high on the SAT. She took IQ tests for fun. You couldn't pay me to take an IQ test, and my score on the SAT was so abysmal it's a miracle I made it into college.

When I was younger, I thought that being smart would make up for the fact that I was local. Back then, it wasn't cool to be from the Methow. Locals were thought of as simple, uninformed, and a little trashy. It was better to have "discovered the Methow," preferably in your twenties or thirties. The ideal migrant was beautiful, fit, educated, and slightly alternative.

The idea was that if you grew up here, you couldn't possibly appreciate the beauty, the landscape, or the wonderfully liberal community.

Once, when I was working at the bakery in Twisp, a guy asked me where I was from. I could tell he assumed I was from somewhere interesting. I had a nose ring and blonde hair. I wore Birkenstock sandals and a blue hippie dress.

"Bridgeport," I told him.

"Oh, Connecticut. That's a nice state."

"Actually, the Bridgeport down the road. The one by Brewster."

His face fell as he realized he wasn't talking to the person he thought he was. "Oh." He scratched his head and reached for his bagel. "I see. Nice to meet you." He hurried out.

If it was bad to be from the Methow, it was worse being from Bridgeport.

Bridgeport is a little agricultural community on the banks of the Columbia River about an hour away from Twisp. Originally built to house workers for Chief Joseph Dam, Bridgeport became an orchard town. Everyone either owned an orchard or worked in an orchard, except my dad, who was a journeyman electrician for the Bonneville Power Administration and turned raw hydropower from the dam into usable energy for most of the West Coast. During the 1980s, migrant workers from Mexico arrived for the fall harvest. Eventually, they brought their families who stayed and bought orchards of their own. Today, Bridgeport is 98 percent Latinx, and if you take a stroll down the main street you'll see *quinceañera* shops, *pan dulce* bakeries, and brightly painted taco stands. It's a very cool town if you're an anthropologist specializing in migration studies, but it's not a place you want to be from in the Methow.

So I worked hard in school. I went on for a master's degree and a PhD, although I didn't really need these degrees. But as a local girl who'd spent her life waiting tables and cleaning houses, I had something to prove. I didn't really appreciate my background until I met a man named James Donaldson and started going to Study Group.

Study Group changed my life. James did, too. I met James while conducting interviews for my master's. His name arose again and again in conversation.

"Have you met James?" people asked.

"No."

"You should really talk to him."

When I finally met James, he terrified me. He was a small man, stooped over with age, but his eyes shone fiercely blue. He would look at you without blinking, which made me feel like he was peering into my soul. Which he was. Graciously, James agreed to an interview, but somehow during the conversation he instead managed to get me talking. I talked so long the sun set and my tea grew cold. When I stood to go, I realized I'd learned nothing about him, but he'd learned a lot about me. That was one of his specialties.

I learned bits and pieces about his life over the next ten years. James moved to the Methow when he was in his early forties. I guess you could characterize him as a hippie. He was ahead of his time on many issues—gender, sexuality, climate change, racism. He was a radical bent on social justice and change. He moved to the Methow along with the 1970s migrants, settling up Libby Creek on a communal farm with several others. Some of the locals found him dangerous. They didn't like him, probably for his sexuality and politics, but to those who loved him, James was larger than life. His mission was living close to the earth and reimagining an earth-centered spirituality.

I'm not sure what he did for a living, but James was not a rich man. He didn't have a trust fund. He farmed garlic and kept goats. Eventually, he moved off the farm and got a second master's degree in counseling. By the time I met him, he was a Jungian psychologist whose grasp of the human psyche spanned disciplines and history. He read voraciously.

The first afternoon we talked, I fully grasped the extent of my ignorance. I couldn't follow anything he said. Everything that came out of his mouth had a reference, a philosophy, or a school of thought behind it. I struggled to keep up.

I don't know why James took a liking to me, but he did. He became my mentor. Over the years he plied me with books, which I dutifully read, and asked me questions, which I tried to answer. He sent me articles and letters in the mail. We met weekly to discuss the books he'd given me. Eventually, when he thought I was ready, he invited me to Study Group.

Study Group was a small group of the valley's intelligentsia. They were older. I was the youngest by about thirty years. They were white, and many were male. But they were, and remain to this day, the wisest, most compassionate individuals I have ever known.

Study Group taught me how to think. I'd spent twelve years in higher education by then, but I didn't know how to put theories into context. I didn't know how to articulate my thoughts or how to pull meaning from what I read.

The first book we read together was William James' *Varieties of Religious Experience*. I loved this book. I outlined passages and took notes on pragmatism. I loved his description of ecstatic religious experiences. I loved his careful, scientific analysis and his objective perspective. But I was unprepared for the group.

"Well, I think it's a bunch of baloney," Diana, a flamboyant ex-journalist and banjo player with a mop of mostly blonde hair, said as she shoved the book away and folded her arms.

Her husband, Bill, glanced at her over his glasses and shook his head. "Well, I lovingly disagree, my dear."

"You're entitled to that, aren't you?" They grinned at each other, delighted.

Bill and Diana Hottell had the relationship I wanted. They enjoyed the mild tension between them. They had keen minds. Bill was the academic, slow and meticulous. He read from his notes with great seriousness, peering through the glasses that slid down his nose. Diana, irreverent and opinionated, rolled her eyes and sighed deeply. They had been married for fifty years. They'd travelled all over the world before settling in the Methow, and while they had little by way of serious income, they lived a genteel lifestyle of music, reading, travel, and humor. I was enamored.

Jerry Sparling cleared his throat loudly, which meant he was going to speak. "Well, I think William James does a good job of studying the unknowable."

Jerry towered over me. He had brilliant white hair and the air of a cynic. He'd been a doctor in Seattle, and his medical background influenced the way he read, thought, and punctuated the air with his finger when he spoke.

"You cannot prove or disprove the subjective experience, but nothing—" he paused dramatically. "Nothing in this book points to a God."

Jerry was a passionate atheist.

"But even William James, at the end—admitted he didn't know." Diana leaned back in her chair.

"Yes, but not knowing does not imply belief."

At this point, James Donaldson, ever the negotiator, gently stepped in. "So what is William James trying to tell us?"

I looked around the table. We were sitting in the back room of the Confluence Gallery in Twisp. The red plastic chair dug into my skin. Sunlight poured through the windows. There were ten of us today. In addition to Bill and Diana and Jerry, there were Leahe, Carl, Richard, David, Mike, James, and me. Ten was enough people. I probably wouldn't have to talk.

James turned to me. "Julie? What do you think?"

Good grief. *What did I think?* I had a lot of thoughts the previous night while reading the chapters, but in front of the group, they crumbled. I don't remember what I said, probably nothing significant, but I do remember the way Diana smiled at me afterwards and Bill kissed my cheek.

"So glad you're coming, Julie. Thank you for being here."

I left the group, spinning. The conversation had been magnificent. Better than school. These people talked about the material from a different perspective. They spoke from life experience. Everything they read and discussed was filtered through a rich lens of life—travel, marriage, children, cancer, loss. I would learn some about their lives—Carl's adult children. Bill's childhood growing up near Republic, his years training to become a Jesuit priest. He married Diana instead. I would learn about Mike's search for God and his return to divinity school. But mostly I would learn about their minds. Their thoughts. The way they reacted to ideas. How they felt about the world.

The next book we read was Mary Clark's *In Search of Human Nature,* a 400-page tome on the biological basis for culture. We talked about nature versus nurture, the dual proclivity humans have for altruism and cooperation, versus avarice and competition. We discussed hunter-gatherer societies and enculturation, food sharing, and the traits we share with our primate ancestors. I didn't like this book. I found it preachy and self-righteous, but I loved the conversation that ensued.

"I like the part about stories." Diana usually started with something tangible. Donning her glasses, she read,

> Our brains are story-learning, story-creating organs. ... Stories, narratives, cultural myths, systems of shared meaning, are the mental food our brains and bodies feed upon.

Diana removed her glasses. "See? It all comes down to our stories, which—" she glanced down at the book:

> we cling to. ... So we find in the world, both past and present, that human beings protect the sanctity of the overall, big story that structures their lives.

"Ha!" She thumped the table. "Hence, Yahweh, Creation, Adam and Eve..."

Mike frowned, as if reaching for a thought. "I—I think you're right." When Mike got excited, he stuttered. "It shows that consciousness evolved as a way to read our own emotions. The stories we told around the campfire and the myths and legends we passed down... They became the collective imagination of the group."

Mike was attending divinity school in Portland. He loved Jungian analysis and spiritual texts.

Diana leaned forward. "And these stories are responsible for the worst genocides the world has ever seen."

Richard waved his hands. I didn't know Richard well, but I liked him. He wore brown cardigans and loafers, and he carried his book like a Bible, clutched between his twisted hands. Richard had systemic sclerosis. Sometimes he shook, and his hands curved inward, so it was hard to grasp the pages. Mike reached over and held the book open for him.

"Those stories gave us shared meaning." Richard smiled as he read.

> There developed within our ancestors a third ingrained propensity—a need for shared sacred meaning to give conscious purpose to the life of the group and identity to the individual.

He leaned back. "I think that's quite beautiful."

"It is beautiful. Without our stories, we're lost." Gently, Mike patted Richard's hand.

Diana beamed. Sometimes, I thought I could see tears in her eyes when she was particularly moved.

We stuck to the text in Study Group.

A lot of book groups disintegrate into gossip sessions or an excuse to get together and hang out. This group believed in the sanctity of learning. If we had something to say, it had to relate to the book, and James Donaldson was a master at pulling out our deepest thoughts. The text mattered, and so did our response to it.

I was teaching by this time. I taught mostly introductory classes in anthropology, sociology, and psychology. I also taught cross-cultural studies, gender, race and ethnicity, and biological anthropology. Between the thirteen different classes I taught throughout the year and my study group, I started to develop a mind.

Psychologists like to point out that although we have mapped the human brain and can even see the neural circuits that fire when we think, we have never been able to find the mind inside the brain. The mind is a consciousness. The mind is a collector of thoughts, emotions, ideas, philosophies, memories. The mind develops whether we feed it or not. It is more than the sum of its parts.

Together, we developed our minds, not our brains. The group didn't care that I had a PhD. They didn't care that I was from here. They did care about my children and my increasing anxiety over climate change. They cared when I arrived one morning and told them I was going through a divorce. Their silence was full of empathy. They had all been there in their own way.

◆◆◆◆

One morning, I noticed that Richard wasn't there.

"You can call and arrange to see him if you want," Diana told us. "He's doing okay. His children came over last weekend."

His death came as a surprise. I didn't know him well, but I had loved his smile and the way he talked with his hands, like a conductor orchestrating a musical piece.

By now we had moved on to Sam Harris. We were reading *The End of Faith*, about the increasing fundamentalism of Christianity, Islam, and Judaism. Harris believed there was no room in the modern world for religion. He believed that medieval superstitions handicapped the modern individual, exacerbating ethnic conflict and divisions around the world.

How could you argue with that? And yet Harris seemed to be missing something. Still, I couldn't put my finger on it.

Jerry had little patience for the book. He already knew that religion was the cause of the world's dysfunction. He didn't need to read another treatise by someone half his age. He tapped his fingers on the book's cover, looking bored.

The previous week he had been discovered in his driveway. It was mid-summer, hot. He'd fallen on the way to get his mail and lost consciousness. One of his neighbors saw him lying there and called 911.

"Just a bump on the head." Jerry waved away our questions. "My knees aren't what they used to be."

The next week, he arrived grumbling that his kids wanted him to move back to Seattle. "I told them. I said, 'David, I love you dearly, but neither you nor Ashley want me knocking about your house. I intend to live in my own house and sleep in my own bed. When I go, I go.'"

It was another bright, sunny morning in the back room. Jerry chuckled at the look on our faces. "I think you all know that I have lived most of my life as an atheist. A lot of people think you'd come to Jesus at the end, but I—" He glanced at me. His bushy eyebrows trembled, and his eyes crinkled with laughter. "I have no such inclination. When I look out my window at night and see into the heavens, there is nothing to convince me that a God exists. The natural world is exquisitely empty of such a being. And yet—"

He paused and looked around the room, his eyes suddenly bright. "I find more beauty and mystery in the natural world than any concept or mythology of a supreme being. It is an extraordinary planet. And I have been extraordinarily lucky to be a part of it."

◆ ◆ ◆ ◆

Jerry died in his sleep a few days later. When I received Diana's email, I sat back, stunned. I couldn't comprehend that the man who had described the night sky from his window three days ago was gone. Just like that.

Suddenly, I knew what was missing from Sam Harris' book. He wrote from his head, not his heart. Jerry, the lifelong atheist and doctor, had learned to live from his heart. It wasn't about science or academic inquiry, really. It was about the beauty he saw in natural systems, the wonder it provoked. The curiosity. You don't have to believe in God to believe in people. Jerry had love, and I was determined to find that for myself.

Having left the church behind years before, I struggled with how to raise my daughters. Did I send them to church so they had a sense of the sacred? Should I read them Bible stories so they had some kind of religious context? What is faith, really? Outside of religion, it seemed like a vast world. Where would I find my faith when everything was falling apart?

By now, James Donaldson had become my therapist. Every Thursday at 1 PM I'd arrive at his house with a book in hand. I didn't know any other therapists who assigned books as part of therapy, but James did. I was reading a book by James Hollis, *Finding Meaning in the Second Half of Life*. Personally, I thought thirty-four was a little young for the second half of life, but apparently the existential and marital crises I found myself in were a common occurrence.

At our first therapy session, I couldn't stop shaking. Sobs erupted from my chest. Tears dripped into my tea. Embarrassed, I wiped them away with the back of my sleeve. I was ashamed for James to see me this way. I wanted to impress him, not fall apart in front of him. It felt like my entire world had come to an end. The life I had planned, the identity I'd tried to prop up. I'd worked so hard to appear successful, smart, and happy. Nothing was going as planned.

We didn't start with the divorce. We started with my voice. James photocopied an annotated Webster's Dictionary definition that listed the origins and multiple meanings for *voice*.

"Read this aloud." He sat across the table from me. The lines in his face were grim.

Was it that bad? I felt like he was making a diagnosis. When I read, my voice sounded thin and uncertain.

"Voice: a sound produced by vertebrates by means of lungs, larynx, or syrinx." I looked up. Was this what he wanted?

"Read on." He took a sip of tea.

"Musical sound produced by the vocal cords… condition of the vocal organs." I paused.

"Go on."

"An instrument or medium of expression, as in 'the party became the voice of the workers.' … A wish, choice or opinion openly or formally expressed. The right of expression. Also, influential power."

"What does that mean to you?"

I tried to think. Images of my daughters at home kept flooding my mind. Mia would be coloring at the table. Annika might be making lunch. I bet they had all the cats inside. What would this divorce do to them?

"Um. We use our voice to express ourselves?"

James smiled gently. He leaned back in his chair. "Why do you talk so fast?"

"What do you mean?"

"Your speech. You talk fast, like you're always rushing."

"My mom talks fast. My aunt talks fast. It's genetic."

"Are you afraid when you speak?"

I had to think about this. I was always afraid to speak in public. I was often afraid to speak in a group. I picked at a loose thread in my sweater. "Maybe. Sometimes."

"Why are you afraid to speak in a group?"

I looked at my lap. "I don't know."

"Why does your mother talk fast?"

"She's Swedish. All Swedes talk fast. We drink a lot of coffee too." I laughed, but James did not.

"Did you ever stand up to your father?"

Uh-oh. "Sure."

"Julie, can you describe a time in your life when you stood up to someone?"

I tried to think. Had I? Ever? I thought about waiting tables and cleaning houses. Waitresses didn't stand up to people. Neither did housecleaners. But I was past all that. Wasn't I? Over the next few days, I thought about what James had said. Maybe he was right. I had never stood up to anyone. And when I tried to speak, especially in Study Group, my words came out jumbled and breathless.

◆ ◆ ◆ ◆

By the time I met James, in my mid-twenties, he already had cancer. I knew little about his medical condition, until it suddenly worsened and he went on hospice care. For reasons I never understood, James did not have family nearby. When he got sick, no one came for him. While I was busy figuring out my marriage and my purpose in life, James was struggling with his own fear of becoming obsolete—of dying alone.

I got a call one afternoon in October. James had been living with various friends for the last two years. Members of Study Group had quietly stepped in and formed the family he never had. Peter, Bill, Diana, and Leahe took turns hosting him, feeding, talking, and caring for him.

"Julie?" It was Leahe.

"I just wanted you to know that James died last night."

I knew he was going, but the news took my breath away. I sank onto the couch, clutching the phone.

"It was very calm, Julie. We were all with him for the last few days. He was conscious and funny to the end. He didn't die alone. He was loved."

I closed my eyes against the sudden tears. I hadn't been there for him. I should have.

"It's okay, Julie. He knew how much you loved him."

That week we had a wake for James. More than sixty people showed up. They brought vegan snacks and notebooks full of quotes, poems, and book references that James had imparted to them. We sat around the living room and listened as, one after another, people stood and talked about James. We laughed. We cried. We realized that he was an enigma to most everyone. He'd been an editor, an educator, a hippie, an activist. He'd been at Berkeley with Margaret Mead and even met Thomas Merton at the Abbey of Our Lady of Gethsemane in Kentucky, where Merton lived for nearly three decades. Everyone had a different piece of James' life, but no one had the whole picture. The man who had worked so hard to reach into everyone else's hearts had kept his own to himself.

The last time I saw James it was a quiet afternoon in early October. Steam from my tea curled in the air, suspended in the afternoon light that streamed from the windows. We were discussing *Voices of Chernobyl* by Svetlana Alexievich, reflections from the residents of that disaster. What struck me most about the book was the description of the land. Good, black soil. Fat, brown potatoes. Cow's milk that had to be thrown out. Some people ate the crops anyway. They couldn't see the radiation. They couldn't feel it.

I knew James wanted me to read the book to get ideas for my own writing. He liked how Alexievich used the residents' own words to describe the trauma. No narration. No storytelling. Just voices.

"Are you finding your voice, Julie?"

"Do you think I am?"

Normally James would never answer a direct question. He'd laugh and deflect.

Now he chuckled and reached for my hand. "Yes, my dear. You're certainly on your way."

Tears clogged my throat. "I'm going to miss you."

The words slipped out, childlike. Almost plaintive.

"I'm going to miss you, too."

We looked at each other. His blue eyes smiled. Outside bees buzzed in the Echinacea. We held hands and watched the light fade into evening.

The Red Coats

Some years ago, when the girls were in elementary school, I made them join the Nordic ski team. I thought it would be a fun winter sport. We skied every weekend up Libby Creek, and I was excited at the thought of someone else teaching them to ski. Maybe the coaches would make them go faster and quit whining.

I also wanted Annika to face her fears about the "Red Coats."

The red coats, as she called them, also known as "Nordies," were the kids who did ski team. They wore matching red parkas, and because Nordic skiing is the coolest sport at our school, they were the cool kids. These were the kids whose parents moved here from Aspen and Vail. Some of the parents were Olympic athletes, most of the parents knew Olympic athletes, and all the parents dreamed their kids could become Olympic athletes. It was very serious business.

Annika had deep-seated fears of the red coats ever since third grade. Because we lived in New Zealand when she started school and had tried a variety of unstructured schooling venues such as homeschool, Community School, New Zealand school, and no school, Annika didn't really start school until third grade.

It was a rough beginning. School involved arriving at the same time, every day, with clothes on. Since Annika spent her formative years believing she was a cat (and who was I to question her chosen identity?), she went to school wearing cat ears and a tail. She also growled at people she didn't like. The red coats thought she was weird, especially on ski day.

Ski day was the one winter day when the whole elementary school went skiing. I thought it would be fun. I sent her along in green snow pants and second-hand cross-country skis. Evidently, the plan was for the school to alpine ski, and since Annika had never ridden the chair lift, they left her at the lodge. For the whole day. I didn't find out until several days later. I heard from a friend that she sat by herself under a table and cried.

It's brutal being a parent. Even today, the memory sears my heart. What I wouldn't give to go back to that day and set her up for success. Which is why I insisted she and Mia do ski team. She would learn to ski with the cool kids (who were now her friends) and love Nordic skiing. I was so excited when I got the two red coats. I don't know if all parents want their kids to fit in, but since I had been such an odd kid, I wanted the girls to feel confident and sporty. The coats were a marker—as sociologists like to say—a marker of belonging to an elite group.

The first day of ski team went pretty well. The coaches divided them into groups based on their ability. Mia was with the Penguins, which was fine because she was only in second grade and there were other beginner penguins. Annika was put on the Devo team, shorthand for "developmental." These were the kids who didn't compete in races. All other teams raced. But her friends were supportive and told her it didn't matter, so she seemed okay. The next day went well, and the third and fourth days. They practiced in-track or classic skiing on the trails near Sun Mountain. On the fifth day of practice, I decided I would go along and ski on my own while they practiced. Today was skate skiing. Admittedly, this wasn't our thing. I had only skated once, and the girls had never skated, but I assured them it would be easy and fun.

By 3:30 in the afternoon, snowflakes fell thick and fast. We arrived at the parking lot sipping hot cocoa with chocolate chip cookies I'd brought from home. It felt festive. I gave the girls a kiss and took off on my own. This was wonderful, I thought. What a great idea for a sport. Something the parents can enjoy on their own while their kids get some of the best coaching in the world. It was perfect.

I skied for an hour or so, slogging along in my old metal-edged Fisher classics. I loved my skis. They were twenty years old, and I don't think I'd ever bothered to wax them, but they worked great. No matter where I went, I could break trail, go downhill, duck-walk uphill, those metal edges making me feel invincible. It was getting dark when I heard a soft click behind me. I turned to see five of Annika's best friends flying up the hill. They passed me as though I were standing still, their long hair streaming behind them, their skis gliding effortlessly in perfect unison, their arms bending and poling like ballet dancers.

Suddenly, I felt sick to my stomach. I knew that today had not been a good day. Skate skiing was not like classic skiing, and these kids were good. Really good. I stumbled back to the car, where I found Annika and Mia already sitting inside. I waved goodbye to their coaches, shoved my skis in the back, and climbed into the front seat. Inside was silent. Quietly, I put the key in the ignition and started the car. We pulled out of the parking lot and slowly made our way down the dark corners from Sun Mountain. When I finally stole a peek at the girls, I saw that they were holding hands. Tears slipped down their cheeks. They said nothing but gripped each other's hands tightly.

At last Annika turned to Mia. "Was it as bad…?"

"Worse." Mia's nose was red, and her blonde hair clung to her cheeks.

They cried all the way home. I tried to think of something cheerful to say, but I had nothing. I'd seen the way those girls skied. I understood now.

When we got home, I made toast and tea. We sat in front of the woodstove. Annika and Mia drank their tea, tears still pooling in their eyes.

At last Annika took a shaky breath. "The hill?"

Mia nodded.

"Did you fall backwards?"

"Into Teague. Who fell into Damon, who fell into Rowan. Everyone fell. Like dominos."

"No!" Annika clasped her hands.

"I couldn't get up. I was like a bug on my back. One of the coaches had to come get me."

Annika sobbed. "Me too. I couldn't move. Travis and Ian had to go off in the snowbank to get around me. I held up the whole team. Every single person saw me sliding backwards. I never even moved forward. I didn't ski one inch."

I suppose if you've never tried skate skiing, it wouldn't sound that bad. But if you've ever been that one person to fall off the chair lift and hold up the whole ski hill, you'd understand. They were traumatized.

◆◆◆◆

The Methow is a very sporty place. I've always considered myself a fit, outdoorsy person. I run thirty-five miles a week, ski in the winter, and bike in the summer. But I am not an athlete. In the Methow, you can't just run or ski or bike, you must be either in training for a race, coaching for a race, or recovering from a race. Only the fittest survive here.

This is difficult for me because not only am I a frugal person, I hate gear. I dislike gear of all shapes and sizes, and I dislike buying it because it's expensive. I think I got into running because it's the cheapest of all sports. Your biggest expenditure is your shoes, from which there are a million to choose. But whether you get the ASICS women's GEL-KAYANO 26 or Adidas Ultraboost 20 or the mysterious Brooks Ghost 12s, they're still shoes. You put them on your feet and you run. It's not that complicated.

Biking is over my head. Recently, I went on PinkBike to find a bike for Mia. I typed into the search bar "Women's mountain bike," but that didn't bring up anything. It was too generic. I tried finding a category in which to browse for a bike, but I couldn't find that either. On the righthand side of the page there's an alphabetical list of more than three hundred bike brands. That's just the brand, not the style or number.

Clearly, biking has become too specialized for someone who's proud they know the difference between a road bike (curvy handlebars) and a mountain bike (straight handlebars).

Todd's not a gear nut either. He had a bike someone had given him, but our ram attacked it and bent the frame.

"Does it work?" I asked. I wanted to bike up to the pass before the highway opened.

"Sure. Does yours?"

"I don't have a bike, but Annika has one. I can use hers."

We put the bikes in the truck and drove to Mazama. It was a Saturday in May. We'd heard that the pass would open soon, and everyone had recently posted pictures on Facebook. "Beautiful!" someone gushed. "Worth the ride!"

We parked at Klipchuck Campground, near the gate, and started up the highway. I was cold and a little irritated because Todd kept wanting to stop and enjoy the view. I didn't know how far it was to the pass, but the shadows were chilly and I didn't have a hat. Todd's bike kept making this little screechy sound, and it wobbled when he went faster than ten miles an hour. This wasn't a problem on the uphill, but I wondered about the way back.

We chugged our way up the first few miles, pedal, screech, pedal, screech. Finally, the road broke out into the straightaway near Cutthroat Lake Trailhead. At last we could see the granite peaks and soaring buttresses of Liberty Bell. The spires are a set of rock formations that include Liberty Bell on the north, plus Concord Tower, Lexington Tower, North Early Winter Spires, and South Early Winter Spires. I don't know who named the Concord or Lexington Towers, but to me they don't fit. I wondered why they didn't name them something in Salish or even after Fred Beckey, who made this area famous for climbing.

I glanced over at Todd and smiled. At last, I was having fun. The sun shone on my face. Biking felt good. I could smell the sweet, fresh earth and melting snow. I pedaled harder. This was easier than I thought. Together, we cruised up the empty road, admiring the views and talking about hikes we'd done on the pass.

"Remember hiking up to Cutthroat last year?"

"You mean when Mia and Pepper, the dog, were dawdling and Pepper got lost?"

"No, Pepper didn't get lost. Remember, she got confused because she can't see?"

"Oh yeah. And she started going with another family."

"Yeah, and Mia freaked out."

I laughed. "Well, you know…"

My reverie was cut short by the glimpse of a road bike speeding past me on the left. It was so silent, it looked like a mirage. I startled, tipping sidewise into Todd whose bike immediately started to wobble. "Yikes!"

"Morning, Julie."

I cringed when I recognized Greg from the bike shop. Suited up in goggles, a helmet, and a sleek red bike outfit, he flew past us with a fleet of tourists behind him. "Morning!" they called in unison.

There must have been twenty or thirty bikers. In various shades of brilliant suits, they glowed like a tribe of futuristic pioneers headed for Mars. Cruising by gracefully at a steady fifteen miles per hour, they smiled and waved. We might as well have been standing still.

I glanced at Todd. His face was pink, and the blue long-johns he'd worn under his swimming trunks had holes in the knees. I looked down at my own getup. I was wearing yoga pants with a rubber band around the ankle to keep my cuffs from getting wrapped around the gear shifts. We both wore tennis shoes, which were also our hiking shoes, running shoes, and gardening shoes. Yesterday I'd shoveled manure in these shoes. I could feel the crumbly bits of dirt still wedged between my toes.

I've always been proud of Todd. With his blue eyes and firm, Montana jawline, I think he's the best-looking guy in the Methow Valley. Other people think so too, even straight men. So I've also always felt proud to be with Todd.

But that morning as the road bikers from Seattle zipped by us with their speedy bikes and sleek gear, I suddenly felt ashamed for us. Gear mattered. Annika and Mia were right. Who were we, biking up to Liberty Bell with our second-hand bikes and long underwear?

◆◆◆◆

The thing about gear is that it really does make a difference. I never knew this because I never tried any. Eventually, Todd got a new bike and talked me into buying a used one from his friend's wife. The first time I got on my carbon-fiber fourteen with the supreme shocks and gritty tires, I was hooked. I could finally go uphill. The low gears were amazing. I felt like a super-athlete. I could go downhill, too, without flying off the handlebars because the shocks kept the bike on the road, even when I hit washboard.

I thought about the rest of my attire. Maybe I should ditch the scrunchy socks and my single pair of shorts for a real bike outfit. I tried Googling "women's biking clothes" and quickly learned that the correct term was "cyclewear."

Wow. Cyclewear went into a lot of personal information.

I didn't know what a chamois pad was, but apparently I could choose between a thick gel one and a midweight, light fleece one. I read that I could pad my hot spots and let my body breathe at the same time. I wasn't sure about all this information and found myself slightly embarrassed just reading about it. I glanced around to make sure I was alone.

When I was a kid, I remember wearing cutoffs for just about every activity including hiking, fishing, hunting, swimming, and biking. I don't remember being bothered about hot spots or needing Aerocool™ mesh ventilation. This was a bit much.

To my great surprise, Todd came home one day with a brown bag from Winthrop Mountain Sports.

"What's that?" The way he had it tucked under his arm piqued my interest.

"Nothing." He disappeared in the bedroom and returned later, looking sheepish.

"What was in the bag?"

"Nothing."

The next Saturday we decided to go for a ride around Patterson Lake. I donned my shorts and scrunchy socks and went to find my water bottle.

Todd was messing around in the bedroom. When I walked in to see what was taking him so long, I saw him hurriedly rip the tags off a new pair of biking shorts.

"Biking shorts, huh?"

Todd muttered something about needing some and proceeded to pull on his long underwear and swimming shorts over the new padded base layer.

There's something I find infinitely silly about men's biking shorts. They accentuate skinny legs, and if you have thick legs, that's no better. Then there's the padded butt part, which looks funny too. Biking attire—sorry, I mean cyclewear—looks ridiculous on anyone, even if you're a Marlboro man from Montana. When Todd appeared with his navy blue long johns and well-endowed buttocks, I burst out laughing.

"What's so funny?"

"Nothing." But I couldn't stop. I laughed and laughed until we got to the trailhead and I actually had to pedal.

Suddenly, Patterson Lake Trail—possibly the easiest, flattest trail in the Methow Valley and which I have run many times—became a nightmarish ordeal of balance and coordination.

I forgot that the lake lies on one side with a twelve-foot drop-off. Running, I never paid attention, but biking, my tires kept drifting toward the edge. I'd swerve to the right, overcorrect, and veer back to the edge. I felt like an ant crawling along a clothesline, except I didn't have six legs with which to cling to the trail.

"Just look straight ahead." Todd tried to coach me. "Keep your eyes ahead of you, not on the trail."

"I can't!" My arms were shaking. My heart raced. My front tire kept darting back and forth on the narrow track like a dog sniffing a rat.

A group of Seattle bikers came zipping up behind us. Todd pulled over to let them pass. I attempted to, but my tire swerved of its own accord and I landed in a heap, thankfully against the hillside and not in the lake. The bikers glared and jangled their bells. I tried to tuck my feet out of the way as I lay sprawled beneath the bike, but they had to slow down and pick their way around me.

After the dust had settled behind them, I picked myself up. Todd dusted me off, and we tried again. I went a little ways before my front handlebar started jiggling from side to side. Then my tire would follow, and soon I was swerving left and right like a drunken sailor. Maybe single-track biking was not my thing.

At last we ditched the bikes and went swimming. I felt better diving through the water. On this side of the lake, we were alone.

We swam for a while, floating on our backs and looking up at the sky. I closed my eyes and breathed deeply. The water felt cool and silky. The sky looked like a giant blue bowl. An osprey glided overhead.

Maybe I should get some cyclewear. The website promised that their clothes would make me ride longer and feel stronger. I wondered if they could keep me on a single-track trail as well.

◆◆◆◆

Several months ago, I met with the executive director of Methow Trails Association. We were talking about social equity and how the association was planning to build a new trail between Winthrop and Twisp.

As of now, there are no trails south of Winthrop, and kids in Twisp and Carlton rarely use the trail system at all.

"Why don't local kids use the trails?" I asked.

"We're not sure." James glanced out the window. "Someone donated one hundred pairs of skis to the school so kids who don't have gear can ski during P.E."

I thought about the red coats and ski team. "I bet I know why."

"Why?"

"They don't have the clothes."

"I think you're right." James shook his head. "The right clothes mean everything in elementary school."

I opened my mouth to agree with him, then stopped. Elementary school? Good grief. I was forty-two years old and the right clothes meant everything to me, too.

Clothes are symbolic. They symbolize belonging, one's place in a tribe. If you don't have the right clothes or the right gear, you don't fit in. You don't belong. The Methow is a wonderful place, and I've always been proud to be part of a culture that believes in fitness and health; but these values can be exclusionary, especially if they're not part of your background.

I used to think that tourists and a lot of part-timers were just buying their way into the Methow with their gear and specialized clothing. Today, I realize that they haven't bought their way in, they've *brought* their way in.

In the Methow, almost 30 percent of the kids live below the federal poverty level. This is higher than the rest of the county, which is at 22 percent. I think it's because the local kids who grew up here and stayed are now having children of their own. But as the housing market climbs and the jobs stagnate, local poverty has deepened. With 35 percent of the population over sixty-five years old, we have a wealthier-than-average older population and a poorer-than-average youth population. Some non-profits are attempting to remedy this inequality. And well-meaning second homeowners and donors give hundreds of thousands of dollars to organizations like Room One, The Cove, and TwispWorks. They believe in social justice and equity, but the problem is endemic.

I used to cross-country ski in jeans and a sweatshirt. Who am I kidding? I still ski in jeans and a sweatshirt. I love breaking trail down to the river. I like slogging around on my old skis. I have a favorite pair of jeans that are boot cut so the cuffs act like gaiters. My ankles never get wet. I never think about what I look like when I'm by myself. The ducks don't care what I'm wearing, and neither do the deer. But I sure wouldn't be caught dead skiing in my old jeans in Mazama.

I'd like to think we grow beyond these things as we get older. Maybe some of us do. But like all mammals, we want to belong to a herd, a tribe. Next summer I might just get myself some Aerocool mesh biking shorts. Maybe I'll get a matching cyclewear top. But no matter what clothes I wear, I still won't be a red coat. Maybe that's for the best.

Mishaps

I've mentioned that my father was an avid outdoorsman, and that I grew up backpacking, hunting, and fishing. Being country people, my parents' way of life valued nature as a matter of course.

I doubt they ever read the "leave no trace" pamphlets that came out in the 1970s, but they figured if you packed it in you better pack it out. Before we left a campsite, they made sure my sister and I scoured the ground for any wrappers, pieces of gum, matchsticks, or food scraps. They taught us how to go to the bathroom in the woods and why you don't pee in lakes or streams—ever. They taught us to value wilderness as untouched by humanity as possible, which is why you don't carve your name in a tree or cut corners on a trail.

My dad was also a woodsman. He knew how to read a map, how to tell the time of day, how to start a fire in the rain, and never to assume you'd catch fish. You always brought food in case you didn't. My faith in my father's ability in the great outdoors was unshakeable. Since Dad was the man in my life when it came to nature, I greeted other men with a bit of skepticism. Did they know how to read the clouds for tomorrow's weather? I thought not.

Shortly after I met Kenny, Dad decided that the three of us should go backpacking. This was not just any backpacking trip, but a five-night journey into the Pasayten Wilderness to a place I will simply refer to as Saddle Lake.

There were two ways in. You could take the Middle Fork or the ridge route. The Middle Fork wound its way along the Middle Fork River for about twelve miles before leaping up an avalanche chute for a straight 3,000-foot vertical climb. Dad and I had hiked this the previous year. It was long, hot, and steep. By the time we crawled into camp, I thought Dad might be dying. He lay on the ground for an hour, gasping, "Never again."

So this time, we decided to take the ridge route. Since I had to work, Kenny and Dad hiked in first. I would meet them later in the week.

Although I hadn't taken the ridge trail before, it looked fairly self-explanatory on my map. I spent the day traipsing along a nameless trail that skirted peaks, dove over cliffs, and cat-tracked its way along the spine of the Cascades. It was alternately breathtaking and insufferable.

Hiking is boring and hot. Hiking with a pack is torturous. I don't think anyone actually enjoys backpacking. Your calves burn on the uphill; your quads burn on the downhill. Mosquitoes feast on your blood in July; horseflies take over in August. In September, you freeze in the morning and broil in the afternoon.

Anyone who says they love backpacking loves the memory of backpacking, not the actual doing of it.

When I finally limped into camp that evening, the smell of fried fish and campfire smoke greeted me. Sunlight lit the craggy peaks around the lake. I heard the quiet splash of fish jumping across the lake. I took a deep breath. Perfection.

Kenny and Dad were on day three of their trip. They'd feasted on huckleberries, rainbow trout, and trail mix. Kenny had explored the peaks around the lake a thousand times and exhausted Dad's conversational skills. They had fished, napped, and slapped enough horseflies to bore themselves nearly to death. They greeted me enthusiastically.

"Julie!" Dad leapt to his feet. He wore white socks pulled up to his knees and a pair of Teva camp sandals. "Got some fish going." Dad adjusted the temperature on the jet fuel stove.

"Sounds good." I shrugged off my pack and collapsed on a log. "That was some hike."

"Did you see the rock cairn on that last pass?" Kenny pushed his glasses up and crouched before the fire.

"Yeah. I almost went the wrong way. That was kind of confusing."

I often got lost in the woods. I'd gotten lost the year before in Nepal and just the previous week trying to find a trailhead up Twisp River. I got lost in parking lots, grocery stores, and anywhere else the scenery looked repetitive. Being lost was such a common occurrence, I was genuinely surprised to have ended up at the right lake.

"Yep, that side trail goes right down into the East Fork. Thick as hairs on a dog's back down there." Dad flipped a couple fish on a plate and handed it to me. "Better watch that on the way out."

We passed the next few days fishing, climbing the peaks around the lake, picking huckleberries, and playing cards. Kenny taught me Kings in the Corner.

I wasn't a card person. I usually read a book or wrote philosophical thoughts in my journal, but Kenny had the energy and enthusiasm of a puppy. He was excited about everything—even the number of mosquitoes he'd killed over the last five days.

"Three hundred and eighty-seven," he announced the night before we left.

"Well, I'm off to bed." Dad yawned. "What time do you kids wanna leave in the morning?"

"I don't know." I shrugged.

"How about I pack up and leave when I want to, and you and Kenny come along when you're ready?" Dad replied. "I'll be a lot slower than you two."

"Okay." Kenny and I shrugged. "Sounds good."

In the morning, we made coffee and the last of the oatmeal. Dad's stuff was gone, so we assumed he'd left at sunrise. We took our time packing up and wandering around the lake. By the time we hit the trail, the sun was high in the sky and the morning was already hot.

"We'd better hurry." I glanced at the sky. "Good thing Dad's slow. I bet we catch up with him by the pass."

We hiked quickly, enjoying the views. We hadn't seen anyone in five days. Not a soul in the wilderness except us, which was perfect. In 1997, by the first week in September you could usually count on having the backcountry to yourself. Except for the high buck hunt later in the month, few people ventured out after Labor Day.

It took us about an hour to reach the first pass. "This way," Ken pointed up the trail.

"No, it's that way." I pointed down the other side.

"No, remember? Here's that pile of rocks."

"Oh." I studied the rocks dubiously. I didn't trust him. "You're sure?"

"Yes. That trail goes down in the East Fork. Remember what your dad said?"

"Right. Okay." Shrugging, I hoisted my pack tighter. "Thought we'd run into him by now."

"Yeah, me too." Kenny slapped at a horsefly. "He must be cruising."

We trudged up the trail, watching for boot tracks. After another couple of hours, I started to worry.

"I can't believe we haven't caught up with Dad." I scanned the trail ahead. It wound through an alpine meadow before zigzagging up to the next pass. I figured we'd gone at least six or seven miles. We should have met him by now.

All afternoon, we watched the horizon, expecting to see Dad around every corner. We couldn't remember when we'd last seen his boot tracks in the dust. By evening, as we slogged up the last incline before Harts Pass, I started to panic.

"He's probably at the truck." Kenny tried to reassure me. "Maybe he's faster than you think."

"Dad's not that fast," I panted.

When we made it to the old blue Dodge, the driver's seat sat empty. I couldn't believe it. It was late. The sun had set. Shadows formed in the valleys, and a cold wind picked up. I imagined that Dad had had a heart attack and fallen off one of the ridges. I shivered. I was too young to lose my dad. Where could he be?

"I bet he just got turned around," Kenny said.

"My dad would never get lost." I was adamant. Dad was a true mountain man. He must be dead. That's all there was to it.

◆ ◆ ◆ ◆

By the time we got to the farm, police lights flashed in the driveway.

"Do you have your husband's dental records, ma'am?" An officer stood in the kitchen with his notepad. His beeper crackled.

Another officer turned to me. "When did you last see your father, miss?"

"Last night."

"You didn't hike out with him?"

"He left before us." I glanced down at my hands.

"What time was that?"

"I don't know. We were sleeping."

The officers made some calls from the house. Mom tried to get us to eat. She made a plate for Kenny—pork chops and dilled potatoes, applesauce, and pie, but I shook my head.

At last, they turned to us, frowning. "You'll need to meet us up at Harts Pass at 5 AM. We got a search party. You," he pointed at me and Kenny, "will stay at the trailhead in case he comes out. We don't want to miss him."

◆ ◆ ◆ ◆

We were at the trailhead before 5 AM, shivering in the back of Dad's truck. Stars glimmered overhead, and a faint band of light glowed along the horizon. The search and rescue team arrived in two pickup trucks and a stock trailer. Kenny and I watched as they unloaded the horses and disappeared down the trail. We listened to the echo of hooves until they faded away. We were alone.

"I don't know why we couldn't go with them." Kenny jumped off the tailgate and paced back and forth.

"Because Dad might make his way out and someone would have to be here."

"I know, but still." Kenny shook his head and gazed wistfully down the trail.

We sulked for most of the morning. We shivered and stomped and blew on our hands until the sky turned pink and the sun rose. I tried to sleep in the back of the truck, but the bed was hard. Bits of manure and alfalfa clung to my hair. I brushed them off.

Now it was hot. The sun shone high overhead, and still we waited. Horseflies nipped at my legs.

Suddenly, Kenny pointed. "Look!"

I peered down the trail. Sure enough, there was movement. Holding my breath, I squinted. I could just make out Dad's profile, slouched over the saddle. His shoulders sagged, and his baseball cap tilted a little sidewise. He did not look happy.

When the party approached, we asked Dad what happened.

"Well," he scratched his head. "I got to that pass with the rock cairn, and I headed down over the other side. By the time I realized I'd gone the wrong way, it was almost noon. I should have turned around and climbed up, but," he shook his head, "I didn't want to climb that 3,000 feet back up. Thought I'd find the ridge trail if I kept to the river."

Kenny grinned. "Damn."

"That's what I said late in the afternoon when I knew I wasn't gonna make it out. I decided to climb up that chute and head back to the lake. I was making good time this morning too—if it hadn't been for that damn horse."

"What about the horse?"

"Search and rescue crew made me ride out. Wasn't two minutes before that crazy horse smashed my knee into a tree." Dad rubbed his knee. "Hurts like a son-of-a-bitch."

I frowned. "Wait, Dad. You're saying you went the wrong way?"

"Yep."

"But you knew about that trail. You told me about it." I couldn't believe that my father had lost his way in the woods. It was a sobering moment. If my dad could get lost, the world was not what I thought.

◆◆◆◆

Dads are good at knowing stuff. The next dad I would meet who knew as much as mine was Todd's, my father-in-law, years later. By then I was thirty-seven, but the moment I met Lee Eberline, I felt like a little girl. Lee had twinkling blue eyes and a bushy mustache that quivered when he talked. I like to think he fell for me as a daughter, the way I did for him. Instant and unequivocal. It helped that he drank coffee.

Lee peered over his glasses at me. We were standing in the kitchen of Todd's childhood home in Montana. Outside, the setting sun turned the sky a brilliant orange. "Got a question for you."

"Yes?"

"Do you take half-and-half or cream?"

Only in Montana and New Zealand did they believe in cream over half-and-half. I was smitten. "Cream."

Lee grinned. This was my first time meeting Todd's parents, Lee and Rita. I had been dating Todd for about eight months, and I wanted to make a good impression.

"Say, Todd." Lee spread a map across the countertop. "What do you say we go to Scott's Lake tomorrow?"

"That one above Esslar?"

"Yep. Always wanted to get up there."

"There's no trail."

"Nope, but you can see it on the map." He tapped the map with his finger.

Todd looked at me. "What do you think?"

"Sure." I smiled. I hated untrailed lakes, but for Lee, I would do anything.

Todd and his dad stayed up late making plans. It sounded complicated.

For some reason, we had to take four-wheelers up to Esslar Lake, then hike the rest of the way. There was lunch to think about and the trailer for the four-wheelers, and fishing poles and tackle. Four-wheelers seemed extreme to me, but I had a feeling that in Montana everything involved a gun and a machine.

◆◆◆◆

We left at the crack of dawn. As we barreled down the highway in Lee's pickup truck, I watched the sky turn gold. Empty fields receded into blue hills as we turned right on a dirt road and wound our way up into the foothills. Sandhill cranes flew overhead. Rivers glittered in the distance.

Suddenly, we ground to a halt before a fast-flowing river. Now I understood the reason for the four-wheelers. The road was impassable.

Todd spent a long time teaching me how to drive the four-wheeler, but I was half listening. The mixed scent of juniper and sagebrush wafted on the breeze. Sloping peaks rose in the distance.

A jackrabbit darted under some sage, and far away I heard a grouse beating his wings.

"Got it?" Todd looked at me.

"Yep."

"You're sure?"

"Why, aren't you driving?"

"Well, only if you don't want to."

"I don't want to."

"You're sure?"

"Yes."

Lee gunned the engine of his machine, and I slipped onto the back seat of Todd's. Putting my arms around his waist, I held on as we descended into the river.

"Is this safe?" I yelled above the engine.

Todd laughed. For a long moment, I felt the tires leave ground. We drifted. Finally, the rubber found ground again. Dripping, we tore up the opposite side of the riverbank.

Ahead of us, Lee waved and pumped his fist in the air. "Whoo hoo!"

We ground our way up the mountain toward Esslar Lake on a cat-track. It was not a trail and certainly not a road. In some places it was so steep we had to stand and lean forward to avoid falling backwards off the machine. By the time we made it to the lake, ripples glittered in the late morning light. A few fish jumped. Above the lake, a rocky peak slanted into the blue sky. We stashed the keys under the four-wheeler, and Lee took one last look at his map before shoving it in the pack.

"Pretty sure we follow this ridge."

Lee went first, followed by Todd, then me. We tramped through the forest before side-hilling up a 1,000-foot ridge. Sunlight shone in patches through the pines. A breeze cooled my face. The Rockies seemed different than the Cascades. They were older and less jagged, but much higher. The air felt thin and cool. I glanced back at the lake. Esslar sat at 10,000 feet. I wondered how high Baldy Peak was.

Trailing behind, I let my mind wander. Lee was an electrician, just like my dad. He had worked in Alaska, been in the Navy, and spent time in Vietnam. He had the air of a man who's done just about everything there is to do in the woods. And like my dad, I trusted him completely.

We made it to Scott's Lake by mid-afternoon. A breeze stirred the water, and dragonflies buzzed the surface. Todd passed out Rita's sandwiches and carrot cake. We munched happily, talking about the peaks, the weather, the fish.

At last, Lee brushed cake crumbs from his flannel shirt and stood.

"Well, looks like it's about time to head back. This way."

"Really, Dad?" Todd studied the forest below us. "We came up that way."

"Yeah, but if we follow this valley, we'll run right into Esslar. We don't have to go the same way we came up."

We trudged downhill in the general direction of Esslar. I daydreamed about Rita's carrot cake. She put raisins in hers. Maybe I should put raisins in mine. A cup of coffee sounded good, too. A fly landed on my arm. I shook it off. We walked and walked, down through a dark forest, then out into an open field.

"Say, Dad," Todd scratched his head. "Are you sure we're going the right way?"

"Yep." Lee nodded.

"Because we should be at Esslar by now."

"Probably around this knob there."

Todd stood for minute, thinking. "Dad, see, that's Old Baldy there, right?"

"Yeah."

"And Esslar is always just under that rock outcropping, right?"

"Yeah."

"So, that outcrop is way to the left."

Lee scratched his head. "Uh. Huh. I don't think so. It's gotta be this way."

I watched the two men negotiate. I could tell that Todd was exercising great patience. He kept glancing back at me as though I should say something, but I had no idea. I was just along for the ride. I knew one thing. I had no desire to backtrack up the mountain we'd just come from. It was evening now, probably around 6 PM. My stomach rumbled. I hoped we'd be home in time for dinner.

After another hour or so, Lee stopped.

"Todd." He scratched his head and looked back at Old Baldy. "I think you're right."

Todd sighed. "Yep."

Lee turned to him. "Son of a gun. I can't think how I got it wrong."

"It's okay, Dad." Todd patted his arm.

"If we keep going, we'll come out below Esslar."

"That's what I was thinking."

We trudged on, while the evening deepened into shadows. I certainly hoped we wouldn't have to spend the night out here. I only had a sweater. I didn't want to complain because I could tell Lee was embarrassed at having gotten turned around. He kept shaking his head.

"Just don't know how that happened," he said to himself.

At last we came to a dirt road, and Lee stopped. "Why don't you guys go on without me? You're faster. You can get the four-wheelers and meet me at the truck."

Suddenly, I snapped to attention. "What?"

Lee looked apologetic. "I've had two hip replacements, and my legs ain't what they used to be."

"You want me to drive the four-wheeler?"

"Yep."

Suddenly the adventure took on a new twist. I had never been on a four-wheeler until this morning. There was no way I was driving that thing down. I shook my head.

"You'll be fine!" Lee called, waving us on.

By the time we arrived at Essler where we'd stashed the four-wheelers, it was dark.

Todd started the engine. "Remember what I showed you?"

"No."

"You'll do great. Follow me."

My hands shook as I pressed on the gas. The road was impossibly narrow. Boulders jutted up like mine fields. I crawled and inched the machine over each one. My heart pounded so hard I thought I might faint. At one particularly narrow washout, I killed the engine.

"Todd!" I shouted. "I can't do this!"

He waved and grinned.

"No!" I shook my head and folded my arms over my chest.

Todd jumped off his machine and ran back. "Doing great, sweetie!" Bracing his two feet behind me, he grabbed the handlebars and maneuvered the four-wheeler over the ledge, then left me on my own.

By the time we made it back to the truck, I was shaking so hard I couldn't move. Lee beamed. "I knew you could do it! A true mountain woman."

Todd cupped my face in his hands and kissed me. "You're the best."

◆◆◆◆

When I think about most of my adventures in the wilderness, they're connected to family. My dad, early camping trips with my grandparents, my mom. Now I go out with my kids.

Mishaps make the best stories. We tell them again and again. They're like dessert. Delicious and fun. We all know how they turn out, but we wait for the punchline anyway.

I had no idea that day at Scott's Lake would be my first and only adventure with Lee Eberline. Five years later, he would die suddenly from brain cancer.

I often think about that day and wonder why we didn't do it again.

I guess we were too busy taking care of everyone else in the family—kids, Todd's mom, his grandma. I miss the father-in-law I had for too short a time.

I'm older now. I know that my dad can get lost, as easily as I can. And that we couldn't see the tumor quietly growing in Lee's brain that made him forget where he was.

I know now that those adventures were priceless, that the mishaps I shared with my dad were the basis for everything he had to share with me. If I could go back to those days in the mountains with Dad, I would. I would tell him it was okay to get lost. I'd tell him I was proud of him anyway. I would tell him that I was okay, too, that I had a man in my life as reliable and steadfast as he had always been for me.

I'd tell him that I loved him forever.

Belonging

Not long ago, my husband and I were invited to a birthday party for a couple who had moved to the Methow nine months prior. The email invitation felt personal. It was addressed to me and Todd specifically, so I was surprised at the number of cars parked alongside the road. Walking up the driveway, I couldn't believe the crowd. More than one hundred people—many of whom I knew, and many of the most socially prominent (and wealthy) people in the Methow.

Shrugging off our coats, we entered a room full of dazzling views and handcrafted woodwork. People chatted animatedly in little groups. Grabbing a glass of wine, I overheard two women talking about the non-profit they worked for in Seattle. They'd been neighbors on Capitol Hill and both ended up here! A group of men was talking about software companies. Snippets of conversation drifted over me as I searched for a group to approach.

"Have you biked the new trail they put in off Thompson Ridge? I did it last week. Not bad. Sixteen miles."

"Oh, Trevor went to Oberlin, too. He loved it."

"We went to Besalú last spring. When are you going?"

Nibbling on the tastefully arranged hors d'oeuvres, I thought about how the social identifiers in this room had changed. Ten years ago the conversations might have been about who'd bought whose land on the East Side road, which kids were in the same grade at Liberty Bell, what they thought of the new English teacher. Today, it was all about firms they had worked for in Seattle, obscure places they all seemed to have been, and how many miles they'd put in on which trails. Ten years ago we'd have talked about life in the Methow. Tonight everyone seemed to feel the need to establish their social class connections beyond the Methow Valley.

There was something else that needled me. Glancing around the room, I couldn't help but wonder how in the world the hosts got to know this many people, this fast? Obviously they were wealthy and athletic—that helped, but... really? I knew all the people here, and it had taken most of the last thirty years to do so.

◆◆◆◆

Belonging is something I've taken for granted. Growing up, I knew I belonged in the Methow. It was home, and the complex web of social relationships was based on diversity and living in a small community. While it may sound odd to talk about diversity in a valley that is 96 percent Caucasian, the Methow used to thrive on difference. There were the church people and the Republicans—the ranchers, the old-timers. There were the Mazama yuppies and the Twisp River hippies, and the organic gardeners, and the Nordic skiers and recreationalists. Everyone was connected in some way, whether you wanted to be or not. We often started a conversation by asking someone where they were from and where they lived. Being from Seattle and living in Mazama placed them in a particular class. Being from the Methow and living in Twisp put them in another. In many ways, this kind of social identification was not about building walls, but rather an attempt to understand where someone was coming from in order to find common ground.

Going to the local brew pub on any given night, you could have a beer with a rock climber turned schoolteacher, a Republican rancher and school board member, or a Twisp River hippie who made her own leather outfits. The diversity that existed in the Methow was based on people from widely varying backgrounds who worked to find common ground. I think of this as true diversity. Diversity isn't a quota or how many non-profits do equity work. Diversity in a small community is knowing your neighbors and working to get along.

Most people want to belong. And part of the draw, the idyll, of rural communities is being enmeshed in the social fabric. New residents join boards, volunteer, and say yes to every invitation. Several years ago, I met a couple who had just moved to the Methow. They enthusiastically posted pictures of their move on Facebook and wrote about how much they loved the local community. Looking at the tags on their Facebook post, I knew that their newfound friends were just-landed residents themselves. This couple fit the Methow stereotype like butter on bread: athletic, early forties, upper middle-class, and expecting their first baby. The valley welcomed them with open arms.

In some ways, I love that the Methow feels warm and welcoming for the just-landed. Rural communities can be suspicious and xenophobic to outsiders. Part of me wonders, however, how much of a honeymoon that welcome is really. Like living with family, being in a small community for the long haul is hard work. Life doesn't go as planned. People lose their jobs. They get divorced. Spouses die. Children struggle.

Being part of a community is more than dinner parties and Nordic skiing. The '70s migrants understood that you can't buy your way into a web of relationships that existed before you arrived. You wait. You coexist. You show up when the opportunity arises.

◆◆◆◆

When Ken and I and our girls moved to New Zealand in 2006, I began to appreciate home in a different way. Although I'd traveled and done fieldwork in different countries, I'd never been gone for so long, and certainly not with small children. Arriving in a different country with a three-year-old, a three-month-old, and $300 in our pockets quickly felt less like a grand adventure and more insane by the minute.

We were shocked at the prices (seven dollars for a cup of coffee) and shocked at the cold. The vernacular confused us: nappies, jumper, dairy, postie. What was kumara, a tog, or a flat white? The light switches snapped instead of switched, the cheese was white instead of orange, vegetables were sold by the kilo, and so on.

The first few weeks were hard. With my usual attention to detail, I had neglected to check the university's annual schedule, assuming it was the same as the U.S. Not so. We arrived in September, which was more than halfway through second semester and almost the end of the school year. There were no apartments available, and the family housing the university had promised did not exist. Jobless, carless, and quickly maxing out our credit card, we canvased the city daily, walking from one end to the other to set up a bank account, meet with my supervisors and admissions, and so on.

One Sunday felt particularly grim. We'd spent the morning walking three miles to the library to check our email and on the way back to our hotel, it started to rain—hard.

"Let's run." I grabbed Annika's hand. Mia bounced against my belly in her Ergobaby carrier. As we hurried down the street, we spied an old stone church with the door ajar.

"Is it open?" Ken squinted through his fogged-up glasses.

"I think so." Shaking rainwater, we ducked through the opening.

Inside, organ music drifted through the darkened sanctuary. Stained-glass windows framed the wooden pews where a dozen members sat scattered throughout the first two rows. A man in a black suit and tie stood reading from the Bible in Samoan. His dark curly hair was flecked with gray, and his face shone under the overhead lights. Suddenly, I realized that everyone in the audience, from the large aunties in their long dresses and hats to the men in suits sitting to their right, was Samoan. Several members craned their necks to peer at us curiously.

Without missing a beat, the man reading from the Bible spoke in English, "A special welcome to the American family who has just joined us. Please, sit down." He gestured towards the front.

As we filed into the pews, the old wood creaked. "What are we doing, Momma?" Annika whispered loudly.

I laid my jacket over her tights and wiped the rainwater from her face. "Shhh."

The service, which took place entirely in Samoan, went on and on. Recognizing the hymns from their melody, I tried to mouth the words. As my shivering subsided, I let my gaze drift to the different scenes on the stained-glass windows. Never had I felt so ill at ease or out of place. I didn't want these people to think we were crashing their party or being culturally insensitive. We were just trying to get out of the rain. The more I thought about it, the insanity of the entire New Zealand experience grew. Maybe we should give up.

By the end of the service, I was planning my withdrawal from the university and wondering how much plane tickets would cost to get home. As we stood to leave, the man who'd given the sermon made a beeline for us. "You will stay for tea." He pointed to another building across the lawn, where women bustled around with paper cups and trays. It was more a directive than an invitation.

Tea consisted of a large and sumptuous all-day potluck. Young men shoved tables together and women piled them high with platters of ham, sweet potatoes, seafood, potato salads, tubs of Kentucky Fried Chicken, French fries, bowls of taro, and steaming vegetables I didn't recognize. The highlight of the meal was pāua, a black oily substance and, as I would learn later, a Polynesian favorite derived from the beautiful abalone shells with the iridescent interior.

I never developed a taste for pāua, not that afternoon nor during the weeks or months that followed, with Sunday dinners first at the church and later at Ninevah's house. Ninevah, the Samoan elder who invited us to tea, had been the family *matai*, or chief, in Samoa. He immigrated to New Zealand in his early twenties, followed by most of his family—including his siblings and cousins and all of his children and grandchildren. They lived within two square blocks in South Dunedin and became the large, extended family that adopted us into their lives.

Over the next three years we joined them every Sunday as well as for Christmases, Easters, countless birthday parties, and White Sunday—the sacred Samoan holiday that commemorates the smallpox epidemic in Samoa, and into which we stumbled that first rainy Sunday morning.

Over the months and years that followed, we grew to know Ninevah and his family well. Ninevah always said that Samoans knew who they were. He said this regarding their relationship with other New Zealanders, who were often racist and hostile toward the immigrant communities in their midst. And he said this whenever discussing politics, especially about American Samoa. "We know who we are," he said. I wasn't sure what he meant by this until one day I asked him.

"Samoans remember their land. We have the ocean, the fish, the plants, our mountains. We know who we are. Even here," he pointed out the window at the gray, sullen sky above Dunedin. "Samoans know who they are. We are Samoan first."

I thought I knew what he meant because I, too, had a home. I had grown up in the mountains, camping, hunting, and fishing with my dad and his extended family. They weren't exotic and there weren't as many as the Samoans, but our family reunions in Oregon numbered around one hundred. Even in the Methow, I felt like my roots went deep. I knew about the seasons and the first green shoots that sprouted in the garden. I knew how many cuttings of hay you could expect in a summer and when the salmon would appear in the river. I knew the Sawtooth like the back of my hand, and all the trails up Twisp River and those up the Chewuch, too. I knew which day in March the sun would appear and when you'd be able to smell the earth again. I knew how dark came so early on November afternoons and the stubborn clouds that hovered over the mountains.

Although I loved New Zealand and fantasized about immigrating there myself, I knew it wasn't home. Like the story of the Little Prince who learns that it's the time spent caring for his rose that makes him love it, I felt like the Methow was mine because I grew up there. It had raised me, in a way.

But there was something else. Ninevah's sense of home was deeper than mine. It was based on a belonging and identity that I didn't have.

Part of it was the extended family. The Vaitupus got together every Sunday. Their family was a complex web of relationships and obligations that were, at times, taxing. As the matai, Ninevah often flew to Samoa at a moment's notice to settle some dispute or to take care of his mother. Although they were too private to divulge much about their family troubles, we grew to understand that family entailed obligations. If someone needed a car or a job or a place to stay, even for months or years on end, Ninevah and the elders were expected to step up.

The family was a web of relationships. Complex, cohesive, and always shifting. When one of the cousins got a girl pregnant, the entire family made sure he proposed, and everyone was expected to help with childcare while the girl finished school. An individual's problem was everyone's problem.

◆◆◆◆

Hawai'ians said the same thing.

"We know who we are," a woman told me simply. "We are from the 'āina, the land."

I was doing fieldwork on the Big Island and had just committed a major social *faux pas*. Attempting small talk at a baby shower where I knew no one, I had just asked a Hawai'ian woman what she did for a living.

"We don't ask people, 'What do you do?' That's *maha'oi*. Rude. It's a mainland thing."

Mortified, I apologized profusely, but the woman waved her hand. "Most people aren't proud of what they do for a living. They're landscapers and housecleaners. I'm a maid at the Hilton. But that doesn't define me. Who we are is from this island. We belong."

This, too, I understood.

Having cleaned houses, waited tables, bussed tables, hosted, weeded flower beds for other people, watched their kids, and even tended bar for a living, I understood that the things we do for money don't define us as people. Maybe that's what attracted me to rural Hawai'i for fieldwork. I was finally in a place where people who did the most menial tasks were still the most powerful in their communities.

I thought about how proud I was to get my first teaching job. Finally, I was doing something other than food service. But many people who belong to a place either by race, family, or because they can't imagine living elsewhere do not have the option to migrate up the economic ladder.

This is not to say that people who do manual labor do not make money. They do. In Ka'ū, the richest families are long-standing Hawai'ians who own thousands of acres of land. They may be the ones moving dirt with their backhoes, but their net worth is more than any mainlander.

◆ ◆ ◆ ◆

At the birthday party for the Methow newcomers, I edged towards Todd, who was deep in conversation with a man I vaguely knew.

"You know my wife, Julie?" Todd smiled at me.

"Nice to meet you." The man looked to be in his early fifties, trim, with salt and pepper hair and a three-o'clock shadow. "And what do you do?"

I smiled at the question. Should I tell him I was a housecleaner, a program director, a college professor, or a mother? Should I mention that I used to be a Libby of Libby Creek?

"Lots of things, I guess." I brushed cracker crumbs from my mouth. "Non-profit. I work for a non-profit."

When my daughters were little, I taught them to be proud of their name and of the land they grew up on. They were Libbys from Libby Creek. I also told them (unwisely) that we would never sell Libby Creek—that it would be home forever. Of course, we did sell our home on Libby Creek, and while both girls were devastated at the time, they also acknowledge that, had we stayed, they wouldn't be the young women they are today. Perhaps we all need both belonging and rootedness as well as freedom and anonymity.

I'll never know what it feels like to belong to a place like Hawai'ians do in Ka'ū, or like Ninevah and his family did in Samoa, but the night of the birthday party with one hundred people who I'd fought long and hard to get know, I realized that belonging in the Methow had changed. People no longer belonged because they loved the place or because they were part of the weird, ragtag community that had ditched professional careers to live in a remote valley in the North Cascades. No, people in the Methow today belonged based on their class and access to resources.

I knew one thing. Glancing around the room, I took in the glittering lights, the din of conversation, the clink of glasses. I nudged Todd.

"Let's go," I mouthed.

The Hunger Games

Swanky music blared from the sound system of the Red Barn in Winthrop. A disco ball dangled from the ceiling, casting thousands of white lights around the otherwise dark room. Several hundred people congregated in little groups with cocktails and napkins full of *hors d'oeuvres*. The women wore tight dresses with knee-high boots and Venetian masks on their faces. The men wore suits and sport coats under their matching masks.

I smoothed my skirt and tried to smile. This was my first fundraiser event for the private school my daughters attended. As a parent volunteer, my job was to run the donation station.

Every registered guest was entered in the computer with a spreadsheet to track how much money they gave. We had three cash registers and computers to manage the crowd. Across the room in the lit-up kitchen I could see other parents and caterers running back and forth with trays full of food and cocktails. Bartenders scooped ice and handed out glasses of wine. By the looks of it, this crowd was here to party, and the evening's schedule of events promised not to disappoint.

Over the next hour or so, the crowd got raucous. By the time the big screen flickered and started playing a video of highlights from the school year, accompanied by moving music and pictures of small children and smiling staff, the crowd cheered. After the video, which made everyone laugh and wipe their eyes, the executive director stepped on stage and started to speak. She talked about children and equity. How this school worked to give every child a chance at a quality education. She talked about the need for childcare and how blessed we were to live in a valley that supported everyone. By the time she finished her appeal, the crowd was heading my way.

"Make sure you enter the amount in the system!" the woman manning our station with me yelled above the din. "You have to find their name!"

A tall blonde in a black evening gown with bulging biceps fought her way to the front of the line and shoved a check in my face. "How much should I make it out for?" She laughed. "Just kidding. Can you write it? I can't see."

"Sure." I couldn't see either. "What's your name?"

"You don't know my name? It's on the check. Make it for $5,000." The woman turned away.

I blinked. Five thousand dollars? I squinted at the name on the check. Ah. Yes. A Methow-famous philanthropist. So that's what she looked like. I'd never met her.

◆◆◆◆

The Methow Valley has more non-profits per capita than anywhere else in Washington State. Thirty-seven of our one hundred and ten pay an executive director. The executive directors, assistant directors, program directors, and other administrative jobs make up the bulk of the professionals in the Methow Valley outside the school district or healthcare.

In 2019, I forayed into this world myself, beginning as the new program director for TwispWorks, a non-profit focused on economic development. I was somewhat familiar with non-profits, having served on several boards in the Methow including Okanogan Family Health Centers and the Community Foundation of North Central Washington. As part of my position with the foundation I'd met with most of the non-profits in the Methow, but I was still unprepared for the inner workings of the non-profit world.

Non-profits have their own vernacular and protocols. People use terms like "the ask" and "the give." "The ask" is the sales pitch, and "the give" is the donations collected from the ask, and so on. There are also terms like capital campaign, awareness campaign, and donor recruitment campaign. There are pitch letters and annual appeals and endowment funds and strategic planning. There are MDOs (micro development organizations) and NGOs (non-government organizations) and EDs, PDs, and CFREs (executive directors, program directors, and certified fund raising executives). There's LYBUNT and SYBUNT (donors who gave *last* year but unfortunately not this year, and donors who gave *some* last year but unfortunately not this), as well as all the acronyms for the other organizations with whom you work.

I was particularly mystified over the gifting. There were unrestricted gifts, sustaining gifts, sequential gifts, restricted gifts, principal gifts, major gifts, gifts in kind, and leadership gifts, not to mention donations, support, charitable contributions, and pledges. In short—money.

Money is the underlying tension between businesses and non-profits in the Methow. A business has to make money by selling a product or a service. If they don't do a good job, they'll lose customers and run out of money. A non-profit, however, can ask for money. If they don't do a good job, they can ask for more money. To the average business owner in the Methow this seems like an unfair advantage. Mismanage your finances and spend more than you make? Send out an appeal letter. Want to purchase your own building instead of renting? Run a capital campaign. Don't like the interest rates on your mortgage? Massage a donor.

It was this aspect of non-profiting that I disliked the most. During my brief stint as a board member for a local playhouse, we were instructed to pick five potential donors—preferably people that we knew in the community—and woo them to make a donation to our capital campaign. I was never sure what wooing or massaging a donor implied, but I didn't like the idea of pretending to befriend someone for money. Maybe I was naïve, but it felt fake.

As owners of the Trail's End Bookstore at the time, Kenny and I could barely pay our bills. We both worked full-time outside the store to supplement our income. One afternoon I sat in a board meeting debating what kind of account in which to put their "rainy day" fund of $50,000. I had just finished paying bills at the bookstore. It had been a busy Christmas, but even after finishing the month with $70,000 in sales, we were $5,000 in the red. I couldn't fathom a rainy day fund of $50,000. As a stressed-out, overworked business owner, I was sick with envy. Now they wanted me to contact five people and take them out to lunch.

I didn't have time to take a wealthy donor out to lunch. I couldn't imagine asking them for money. I turned in my resignation that week.

◆◆◆◆

Years later, when I started at TwispWorks, my job was to design programming to support small businesses. As a former business owner, I knew that the main things business owners need are customers and time. They'll never have enough of either. But my job at TwispWorks depended on offering something valuable to the business community. So I developed programming to support businesses. We already had the Methow Investment Network, a local investment group that gave non-traditional loans to startup businesses. I also advertised various workshops and training seminars which we arranged. I knew, however, that few business owners ever have time to complete a seven-week boot camp (as one of our workshops required), and no one wanted more Internet training. They just wanted Internet.

Business owners are an eclectic group. From the forty-something professional who moved to the Methow to recreate to the wealthy entrepreneur who bought a Methow Valley business as a tax write-off, a few business owners are relatively well off and educated. But the majority are not. Most have one or two employees. They make less than $25,000 a year. Running a business in the Methow is difficult. When Highway 20 closes, Winthrop turns into a ghost town. Christmas and a good ski season generally bring people, but the lack of overnight accommodations limits the number of people. In the summer, fire seasons can shut down the valley, with locals and tourists alike fleeing to the West Side to get away from the smoke.

TwispWorks board and the Methow Investment Network were both comprised of savvy professionals, many of whom were recently retired and had just moved to the Methow or owned a second home here. Most of them had some kind of business background and money to invest. But theirs was a different world. Occasionally, I looked up certain investors to see which business or firm they worked for. Many were CEOs and managers of large real estate companies and investment firms based out of Seattle. The websites, with pictures of gleaming boardrooms and good-looking people in suits and ties, emanated money and class. It was a far cry from the hardware store that blared Christian radio or the stores selling tourist souvenirs in Winthrop.

In the Methow, the non-profits exist alongside the business community. Their boards are made up of wealthy donors with experience and resources beyond the Methow. Often, the same people serve on two or three boards. The organizations support great causes: affordable housing, childcare, relief from domestic violence, access to birth control, conservation easements, a food bank, and the arts. Through their board members these organizations have access to those gleaming boardrooms and portfolio funds. Furthermore, the non-profits in the Methow are largely untouched by fire seasons, bad snow years, even recessions or the pandemic. While the non-profits certainly support the community on many levels, they also create a deep inequality when it comes to doing business in the Methow. They operate on a different playing field.

◆◆◆◆

There are a handful of extremely wealthy philanthropists in the Methow. These families choose which organizations to fund based on their interests and background. Over the years they've invested millions of dollars in the community, which has changed because of them. It's why we have a Merc Playhouse and a chamber orchestra festival, art festivals, art galleries, open space, environmental protection, and NGO social services. It's what makes the Methow a desirable place to live. Nowhere else in eastern Washington can you see a play every weekend, attend a concert by a new Portland band, or wander through art galleries.

It's also why there are still big pieces of empty land along the valley floor. Driving from Washington Pass through the valley you can see the influence of conservation easements. The landscape is comprised of homes along the tree line or overlooking the valley floor with hundreds of acres of connecting land between them. This is not without great effort or design. The Methow Conservancy has worked with landowners since 1996 to permanently protect open space in the Methow and to create a wildlife corridor along much of the valley floor.

All of this comes at a cost. In the non-profit world, we call it the Hunger Games. If you look through a pre-pandemic calendar of events in the Methow Valley, nearly every weekend hosted a fundraiser event for a non-profit. These events form the social calendars for board members and prominent families in the Methow. It's hard to find a free weekend to schedule a new event. The non-profits scramble to claim the best weekend for their annual fundraiser. More importantly, they scramble to ensure their highest donors are coming. The Hunger Games are the delicate dance between the non-profits. All thirty-seven of the organizations which pay an executive director compete for the same resources: donors, grants, board members, and volunteers. Their success as an organization translates directly to the amount of money they raise.

The best way to see the Hunger Games in action is by attending a non-profit's annual fundraiser—the event above all others which must shine. At this event, the most prestigious donors will be present. The organization will showcase all that they've accomplished in the past year. They will craft a clear message about their role in the community and why they must appeal for your support.

The late anthropologist Clifford Geertz coined the term "focal institution" to describe any institution that provides a window into the culture. A focal institution is a social institution or event that draws a large number of people and serves to reinforce the social order, beliefs, and values of the group. As sociologist Émile Durkheim demonstrated earlier with his analysis of religious events, a focal institution is a community performance that commemorates tradition and belief systems and reflects the larger structures of society.

My husband, Todd, is the drummer in a band in the valley. Over the years he's been asked to play for hundreds of events. As a mother, board member, program director, and Todd's wife, I get asked to serve or volunteer at just as many events. I've tried analyzing these events from a social science perspective. I've even taken notes in the backroom and jotted down ideas for theoretical analysis. In my master's thesis I called these "marker events" and wrote that these events served as markers of belonging. To see and be seen at an event connotes belonging and place within the community. But lately, I think a focal institution best describes the function and meaning of these events.

Fundraiser events serve several purposes. As I said, they are opportunities to see others and to be seen. They're one of the only opportunities to dress up in the Methow, which is an occasion in and of itself. With 6,000 full-time and 4,000 part-time residents, the Methow is small enough for you to be known, but large enough that you keep adding to your web of acquaintances. To be successful, events must contain the right ratio of people—enough people everyone already knows and enough people everyone wants to get to know.

Reestablishing social connections requires a period of time for alcohol consumption and small talk. This is why people attend events—to see how everyone else has aged, whether they've put on a few pounds or lost them, who is still married to whom, and so on. None of these details are interesting if you don't know the people. There's nothing more tedious than listening to gossip about people you don't know and have never met.

Another function of these events is to reestablish the social order. This is done through the donors who show up and pay for the $100 ticket. They are also the ones who donate or bid in the silent auctions. Donors are not always second homeowners. Many are full-time residents, but they move in the part-time circles. Every non-profit knows that the second-homeowner community is their donor base. It's important not to offend them.

The donors are the target audience. The food, wine, and evening events are designed around them for the purpose of extracting a sizeable donation. Everyone knows this. It's not considered exploitative. Which is maybe what I didn't understand when I was asked to take a donor out to lunch. It's one of those unwritten codes of conduct that establish the social order. Outside of the donors, the people putting on the event, the volunteers, and the locals who come but won't donate are all part of the social milieu.

Annual fundraiser events follow a particular pattern. There's always the meet-and-greet with lots of wine and beer. The schedule of events can vary but usually includes an emcee, some kind of music background, and a video or a story that illustrates the role of the organization in the community. After the video or story comes the ask, which is when people get out their checkbooks. After the ask there's usually some dancing or more music or time for those who weren't sure how much to give to think about it, before the evening comes to a close. Like the altar call at a church service, the ask is the emotional climax of the evening.

A few years ago I attended an annual fundraiser at the Winthrop Barn. It was another crowded event with an open bar and live music. Original artwork had been arranged in a tent on one side of the room for a silent auction. People perused the tent as they sipped wine and chatted in small groups. Room One is a social service organization that provides counseling for battered women, access to birth control, food vouchers, and other forms of help for anyone who walks in their doors. From its inception as a tiny support organization with two women volunteers, it now employs ten people and serves several hundred every year.

On this particular evening Todd played music while I served *hors d'oeuvres*. I was happy with my job. I got to wear a cute dress and tall boots. I got to socialize and see new artwork. I was just admiring a piece by a local construction worker (I had no idea he was an artist) when the music lowered and the emcee for the evening invited a group of young women on stage. I recognized them as my students in Omak at Wenatchee Valley College. Two of the girls were Latina and taking my anthropology class that quarter. The other two I knew from years past. The girls, dressed to the nines in short dresses and heels, took turns speaking about Room One. They told about showing up at Room One and having the staff give them free counseling and support services. After each girl spoke, the crowd erupted with applause.

I smiled and waved. They didn't see me. I'm not sure they would have wanted to. What the crowd didn't know was that these girls were straight-A students from good families. As Running Start students, they were enrolled in both high school and Wenatchee Valley College. One was the president of the student body association, and they had all been accepted at universities elsewhere. Also, they weren't from the Methow Valley. They were from Omak, a community an hour away. Something bothered me about seeing them up there. I couldn't help but feel like their stories reinforced an inaccurate stereotype. I wondered if they agreed to speak to this group because they didn't know anyone from here.

After the girls spoke, the executive director gave a compelling ask, emphasizing the helplessness of these young women and the particular challenges girls face in our society. I got out my checkbook along with everyone else. Conscious of my own privilege for being a white college professor and living in the Methow, I wrote a check for $100.

◆◆◆◆

The role of philanthropy in the Methow is complex. I'm sure it's complex everywhere. In a country where more and more of our basic services are privatized and left up to the individual to secure, philanthropy may be our only option to fund things like childcare, libraries, access to healthcare, reproductive counseling, and housing. But philanthropy is fickle, dependent on the donors' whims and interests. It also reinforces something I'm not comfortable with. I know that I don't fit every stereotype, and neither do most people. Why not emphasize that these girls were going to college? Why not applaud them for getting straight As and working hard? Those girls were multifaceted. They made a good story, but it was a tiny sliver of their lives—not the whole picture.

In his recent book *Billionaire Wilderness*, Justin Farrell argues that the ultra-wealthy use nature as a way to distance themselves from low-income people and to further climb the social ladder. By tying up land in conservation easements, the ultra-rich in Teton County, Wyoming, were able to create a recreational paradise for their own use, whilst being seen as philanthropists throughout the community.

In the Methow this book made a lot of people upset. Personally, I agreed with Farrell's analysis. But with close to eight billion people on the planet, I still think conservancy easements are a good idea. White or not, we need more protected land, not less. His point, however, that the wealthy were "buying" prestige by investing in land and conservancy easements could also be made about the social service organizations in the Methow. Writing a check to support someone you feel is in a different class reinforces that separation, thereby reinforcing the social order. As Geertz suggested, all focal institutions are a microcosm of larger society. He said that within these events the social order is reinforced.

Donors play an important role in the Methow Valley. Without them we would not have the cultural events, the open space, or the services they support. People like me wouldn't have jobs.

I'm not arguing against the non-profits or the positive impact they've had in the Methow Valley. But I am suggesting that the relationship is paternalistic—like the plantation era in Hawai'i, which ensured that those at the bottom stayed there for almost one hundred years. I wish there was something more empowering we could do to help mitigate the increasing divide between the rich and the not-so-rich.

◆◆◆◆

Back at the fundraiser, we were cashing out the credit card donations at the end of the night. The guests in their Venetian masks had trickled out, leaving behind a floor littered with balloons and napkins and sticky with wine and beer. Someone turned the house lights up.

"How much did we make?" The executive director hurried over and peered at my computer screen.

I didn't understand the software system, but the woman working next to me did.

"Hmm. I thought we'd do better than that."

"We still have all the pledges out there. Those should come in over the next week."

"Yes, but it's TwispWorks' Big Shebang next week. Aren't they doing an ask?"

"True. Then there's Methow Arts, and isn't Room One's annual fundraiser after that? If we don't get those pledges before Friday, there'll be too many annual appeals."

"Let's send out a letter on Monday."

The Good Life

When I started my PhD program at the University of Otago in New Zealand in 2006, amenity migration was the academic rage. "Tourism impact studies" were old. Dean MacCannell's "search for authenticity" was out, but leisure and migration studies were definitely in. Amenity migrants, I found, were privileged enough, whether by birth or effort, to afford to move anywhere in the world in search of "the good life."

In New Zealand, the good life happened to be hobby farms all over the countryside, as urban folks from Auckland, Brisbane, or Sydney moved south in search of countryside and the simplicity it offered. The dean of the tourism department had written extensively on the topic, and by the time I arrived the whole department was well versed on the ins and outs of amenity migration.

I was curious about the New Zealand hobby farm. New Zealanders were passionate about two things: rugby and gardening. Rugby remained a mystery, but gardening was something I could handle. Every weekend, we packed up the car and drove to the countryside in search of these amenity migrants and their hobby farms.

It reminded me of the Methow.

Arrowtown, in central Otago, happened to be an Old West theme town, like Winthrop. Wanaka, an hour away, was known for water sports, bungee jumping, and squirrel-suit gliding. The countryside in between was scattered with small farms owned by rich young couples who threw themselves into gardening and raising sheep, chickens, pigs—and worms.

New Zealanders get very excited about worms. They're kept in what might be raised beds for vegetables but are instead covered with old carpets, and are fed garbage. You can buy the worms for $5 a pound.

New Zealanders also love wine, for which they're famous, and peonies, which they ship to Japan during the winter. Everywhere we went, New Zealanders were certain that life in New Zealand was the best possible life on earth.

"Ah, you'll be moving here for good!" they told us. "It's the best place in the world."

That sounded familiar. Scanning through books about the Methow Valley, similar themes emerge: *The Smiling Country, The Methow Valley: Between Home and Heaven, Bound for the Methow, Lost Homeland*, and so on.

I used to be envious of the good life. Back when I worked eighteen hours a day, I didn't have time for a good life. The happy couples who moved here to plant organic gardens drove me crazy. I resented their chitchat about tomato plants and when to plant the corn. I wanted to grow tomatoes. I wanted to own a piece of land and have leisure time myself. Instead, I served them dinner and cleaned up their kids' messes.

Happily, life moves on, and eventually I got to have the good life.

The good life is *expensive*. If you've seen *The Biggest Little Farm* you know that the film isn't exactly realistic. They must have spent $20 million on that farm. You don't plant a circular grove of ten-year-old citrus trees for twenty bucks apiece. I know, because I now have a little farm.

Weird things are expensive on a farm. Irrigation equipment of any kind—no matter how lowly the piece of pipe fitting or a threaded nozzle—will cost $100 a whack. You might spend $300 fixing a leak in your field only to find that that wasn't the problem. You might then have to pay someone to dig up your main water line, only to find that this wasn't the problem either. Five hundred dollars later, you realize it's your pump. When you get the bill for new seals on the pump for $800, and this doesn't do the trick, you must pay someone else to come look at your whole system. By the time you're done, you've spent $3,000 on nothing. One day, the water magically works. You never know why.

This is a true story. Todd is still upset over it. So yes, the good life is expensive.

Shortly after I put in my perennial beds around the house, I realized we needed a deer fence. We had a deer fence of sorts around the blueberry field and the greenhouse, but there was never a need for one around the house until I moved in. Since the flowers were my idea, and since we tacitly agreed to a set of gender roles—Todd did animal stuff and I did flower stuff—I had to put a deer fence around the yard.

I had never put in a fence by myself. I had never dug a post hole. My first afternoon, I suited up in my old jeans, work boots, gloves, and hat. I marked out the new fence with orange paint, then got to work. The first hole was surprisingly easy after I got through the grass. The second hole went okay, and the third. By the fourth hole I was sweating buckets, and a blister formed under my gloves. I staggered in to make dinner that evening with eight holes behind me. The next morning, I could barely move. My arms were sore. My back was sore. My hands were covered in blisters. That day, I only got five holes dug because I ran into the old riverbed.

Fifty million years ago, the river flowed just beneath our house in a curving arc that formed a natural barrier between the rich, alluvial clay that Todd was so proud of, and the stony, stubborn floodplain below it. My fence was slated to go along the natural arc. What I didn't realize was that a riverbed is not conducive for post holes. A riverbed is not what it sounds like. It sounds lovely, soft—a bed for a river. But no. A riverbed is an underground ocean of rocks with sand in between.

My fencing slowed to a crawl. Every day I went out to the fence line and rammed my rock bar into the ground. Sometimes I lay in the field, exhausted. The riverbed had done me in.

The only good thing about fencing is that it gave me biceps. For the first time in my life, I had arms like Jennifer Aniston—tanned, lean, and bulging with muscle. Okay, bulging might be an exaggeration, but even the girls noticed my arms. When I picked them up from school, they were impressed.

"Wow, Mom. You look like Jennifer Aniston."

This was all the motivation I needed. Eventually Dad came to visit, and he and I finished the holes and stretched the wire. At last, my deer fence was complete.

I was so happy. No more would I wake to find the pink blossoms stripped from the decorative crabapple or the first blooms from my roses.

A couple mornings after we'd finished the fence and installed the new gate across the driveway, I made myself coffee and settled on the couch. Todd had just left for work. It was early. The rising sun cast an orange glow across the yard. I smiled and took a sip.

Something moved in the yard. It looked like an antler. It couldn't be. It was. A large, sleek buck calmly picked his way through my flower beds, nibbling on some blue delphiniums. Spilling my coffee, I leaped to my feet, peering out the window. Not one, but three bucks stood in the yard, quietly eating my perennials. I ran to the front porch.

"Yah!" I shouted. "Yah, yah!" They swung their heavy heads around and looked at me, then went back to eating.

Stumbling, I hurried to the office window to check the gate. It was open. Todd must have left it on his way to work. I speed dialed his number.

"Todd, you left the gate open." My voice quivered.

"I did?"

"Todd, there are three bucks in the yard."

"Oh." Silence. "Shoot, I'm sorry. Uh, let's see. Go get my shotgun. See if you can scare them."

I hurried to the gun cabinet. In the background, I could hear the guys talking.

"She's going for the guns?"

"Does she know how to shoot?"

"Is that safe?"

I tiptoed to the back porch, where I had a shot at the deer. "Okay. Now what?"

Todd's voice was extra calm. "Okay, sweetie, so you just carefully—now be real slow and calm. Just breathe."

"Tell her to pull the safety."

"To the right, make sure she pulls it to the right."

"So you just undo the safety. Make sure you're outside. Are you outside?"

I was standing on the deck in my very short pink nightgown. Having grown up around guns, I actually knew what to do, but it had been a while. I rested the muzzle on the railing and reached for the shells. *Click*, they slid into the chamber. *Click, click*. In the yard, the bucks had moved on to the day lilies. *Rip*, they chomped as they chewed. *Rip, rip*.

The safety was a little sticky. "Which way does it go?"

"Tell her to the right."

"No, it's a shotgun. That safety goes to the left."

"Is she actually going to shoot it?"

"Man, should you go home?"

"Sweetie, listen. You gotta move it up, and then to the right. Real slow now. Real slow, honey."

"Okay, I got it."

Silence.

"Well, now, don't—"

Boom!

The shot exploded into the quiet morning. The butt kicked back against my shoulder. When the ringing in my ears cleared, I could hear the guys still on speaker.

"Don't shoot!"

"Did she shoot the deer?"

"Shit."

I glanced at the phone. The bucks had scattered a little way off, but they weren't exactly afraid. They looked around, shook their heads, and moseyed on to the weeping cherry.

I tried another shot. Then another. I was shooting above their heads. I knew better than to hit one, and the commentary from the guys was irritating me. I grabbed the phone.

"Todd, they don't care. It's not scaring them off."

"Okay, honey. Why don't you get on the four-wheeler. You can run them out."

"I don't know how to start the four-wheeler."

"I'll walk you through it."

Furious, I grabbed the gun and ran outside. With the gun strapped across my knees, I straddled the four-wheeler and pushed on the clutch with my bare toes. I turned the key. Nothing.

"You gotta put it in gear."

"Does she know how to put it in gear?"

Fumbling, I turned a bunch of buttons and wiggled the ignition. The four-wheeler jumped to life with a roar. I rammed on the gas and tore after the bucks. Now they did look alarmed as they saw me racing at them on a green four-wheeler with a gun. They turned and trotted towards the river and the deer fence.

Ah, the fence. Now they were stuck. It was a deer fence, after all. The bucks stopped at the fence and looked back at me. *What now?* I didn't have a clue. They stood there as I barreled down at them, pink nightgown blowing in the breeze, clutching the gun. They stomped their feet uneasily and looked at the fence. They turned back to me and lowered their antlers.

Good Lord, they were going to charge.

I killed the four-wheeler and leapt off with the gun. The phone, still on speaker, crackled. I could hear Todd's voice, anxious. "Julie? Julie?"

Fumbling with the safety, I raised the shotgun and took aim.

Although I pretend to be mechanically illiterate, I am actually a pretty good shot. Once, I dropped a kudu in Namibia at three hundred yards with one shot, straight through the lungs.

From the phone, I could hear panic in the guys' voices. "Todd, what's going on?"

"What's she doing?"

Silence.

Fire.

The shot echoed across the field. The buck jumped and whined. Together, almost in unison, the three bucks levitated over the fence, tearing it with their weight. They landed in a disorganized heap on the other side and galloped toward the river.

I stood there for a minute or two, listening to the guys' commentary. Irritating. I decided to let Todd worry a little more before I told him what happened. I clicked the phone off. Maybe next time he'd shut the gate.

◆◆◆◆

The good life is expensive because fences are expensive. It's not the fencing materials so much as it is the labor. After putting up the deer fence, I was pretty sure I could redo all the fences. In a fit of Jennifer Aniston enthusiasm, I redid the garden fence one week while Todd was in Montana.

He went to Montana a lot. His parents were aging, and I understood that it was important to see them. Sometimes I went along, but I couldn't always leave the girls, and I knew his mom liked it better when I didn't come. All the same, I resented his every-other-month trip to Montana. Whenever he left, I was responsible for the animals.

Although I liked the idea of the good life and raising our own meat, I was less sure about actually doing it. Animals are challenging. They're always getting out or tearing something down or going where they're not supposed to go. They eat what they're not supposed to eat. And when you're a five-foot-four female, they're usually bigger than you.

Usually, I have some chore when Todd is gone that requires me to do something mechanical. Sometimes I know exactly what to do, and sometimes I have no clue. Take the irrigation, for example. The irrigation system is impossible for anyone other than Todd. This is a proven fact. However, it is theoretically possible to turn on the gravity without having to start the pump. This is something I dislike very much because it requires a lot of shutting different lines on and off. The lines are all over the property, and none of them turn the same way. They're not the same valves. Some are round like a steering wheel and go to the left. Others are levers and go to the right. And it's not that I'm mechanically incompetent so much that Todd has a way of communicating that confuses me.

It goes like this.

"Okay, sweetie… you're going to turn off the main line."

"Which main line?"

"The main line to the field."

"Which field?" We have three.

"The main line by the blueberries."

Okay. I trudge out to the blueberries. From here there's a big pit with a bunch of pipes and knobs and levers. I kneel down, with the phone on speaker. "Okay, I'm at the main line."

"Great, now turn the knob to the left. Very slowly. Don't wrank on it."

There are three knobs and several levers. "Which knob?"

Silence. "The one I showed you."

"Which one was that?"

"The main one."

"The green one, the gold one, or the blue one?"

"The one above the black plastic thing."

"The gold one."

"Maybe."

Okay. I twist the gold knob to the left. It doesn't move.

"It doesn't go that way."

"Yes, it does."

"No, it doesn't."

Silence. I can always tell when Todd is losing his patience with me. I'm not trying to be dumb. But a tiny part of me is irritated that he's left, once again, in the middle of summer.

"So. What should I do?"

"Turn it to the left."

I try again. It doesn't go to the left. "Todd, it doesn't turn to the left. I can turn it to the right, but it won't go that way."

"Okay, turn it to the right."

Silence.

"I did."

"What happened?"

"Nothing, it just keeps going. I can turn and turn."

Todd sighs deeply.

This can go on for hours. It usually does.

But I like the good life. This summer we have more than a hundred tomato plants in the greenhouse, and a dozen pepper plants and our own melons—cantaloupe, watermelon, and honeydew. We just finished the blueberry harvest, which Todd kindly let Annika have. She sold berries to the Mazama Store and people came for U-pick. She made $2,000 toward her college fund.

We also have kale, potatoes, corn, beets, herbs, carrots, broccoli, onions, peas, summer squash, and one whole field of winter squash. And we have lamb in the freezer, sheep in the fields, beef in the freezer, and three cows in the field.

I'm supposed to grain everyone at bedtime because Todd is once again in Montana. (*Graining* means feeding the sheep and cows grain at dark, so they get used to coming to you. You do this in case they get out, so you can get them back in.) Instead of doing our phone communication thing, I might text him because that leaves a little more ambiguity on whether I have completed the chores according to his directives.

It goes like this:

> Hi Sweetie (heart emoji).... Going to bed. Grained the sheep.

> Great, how about the cows?

Silence. I have specifically not grained the cows. They're huge. And I won't put the sheep in their corral unless the cows are at the other end of the field. The cows have grass. I don't know why I'm supposed to grain them. Instead I type:

> R you going to grain me?

This will distract him.

It does.

> Wow. You bet. What kind of grain do you want?

And so on.

◆◆◆◆

One summer, it was especially hot. Todd had thought it would be nice to have honeybees, so he bought me a hive. As with the animals, I was less than thrilled about honeybees. Honey sounded good. Very granola. Very cool. But I was afraid of bees.

One of our neighbors, a veteran beekeeper named Susie, agreed to mentor me. Susie and her wife lived up Twisp River. She had thirty hives herself and made candles and honey products for the farmer's market. Susie was calm and confident and a badass around bees. She showed me how to open the hive and check the boxes for honeycomb. She showed me how to use smoke to calm them down and to wear white and a bee hat.

By mid-July, it was time for me to check the bees myself. I was waiting for a cool day because I didn't want to accidentally start the field on fire with my smoker. I was just on my way out to the bees when a strange truck came rumbling down the driveway. A man in his sixties climbed out. He had a floppy hat and a pink nose and glasses. His face was flushed with heat. He wanted to know if he could set up his easel and paints in the field. Naturally, I was flattered that he wanted to paint our little section of river, so I said, "Sure." He climbed over the fence and set up under the shade tree in the middle of the field.

That evening, before he left, he asked if he could come again the next morning to finish.

"Sure," I said. "No problem."

When Todd got home, I told him about the artist and the painting and how I needed to check the bees, but I was a little scared.

"I'll do it with you in the morning."

"Really?"

"Yeah, I've done it before."

The next morning when I awoke, I saw that Todd had moved the ram into the north field.

"Todd." I called him on the phone. He was down at the barn. "Why'd you move the ram? That artist guy is coming today to finish his painting."

"Oh, yeah. I forgot. Well, it'll be fine."

It would? We all knew the ram would charge people. I wanted to argue, but whatever. We had to check the bees.

By the time I got outside, it was hot. Sweat ran down the back of my neck under my long, white sleeves. I'd tucked my shirt into my pants and donned a white bee hat which had a screen for my face. Todd came up from the barn just as the artist guy came rumbling down the driveway.

Todd shook the artist guy's hand. "Nice to meet you. Yeah, go ahead and set up."

"The ram is in the field," I reminded him.

"Isn't he lovely." The artist guy smiled. "What a beautiful creature."

I glanced at the ram. I never thought of him as beautiful. Last year the donkey had kicked one of his horns off. The hole from his horn went down to his brain, and we had to fill it with silicone to keep it from sucking air and killing him. The ram, with one horn, looked a little silly and his short coat was brown with dust.

Todd smiled proudly. He loved the ram, horn or no horn.

The artist guy climbed the fence, and Todd and I walked out to the bee field.

"Now, the key is to be calm." Todd strode quickly ahead of me.

I had to jog to keep up. "I know. I did this with Susie."

The air hummed with honeybees. Todd scratched his head. "I thought they'd be less active."

"Well, it's already after nine." I shaded my eyes against the sun. A few dozen bees flew around; most were in the hive. I waited for him to make the first move. "Don't you want a bee hat or a screen?"

"Bees don't bother me."

I watched as he approached the hive. He hesitated before grasping the lid. It was stuck. He gave it a jerk. Instantly, the bees moved faster. Their buzzing got louder.

"Careful." I stepped back.

Todd swatted a couple near his face. "Ow! Shit."

"Did they sting?"

"Yeah. Shoot." Todd backed away. Bees poured from the box. The air turned tense.

Even I knew this was not good. They didn't act this way around Susie. We'd forgotten the smoke. The bees, however, had not forgotten Todd. He dropped the lid and ran. The bees swarmed after him, furious. Finally, he stopped halfway to the river. I didn't know whether to laugh or be concerned.

"Benadryl!" I heard him yell from across the field.

"Okay!"

"Do we have any?"

"I don't know!"

"Can you get some?"

"Now?"

"Yes!"

As I jogged to the house, I noticed the artist guy standing under the tree. His easel sat before him, and he was looking toward the river. Behind him, the ram stood with his nose pressed lightly against the man's thigh. I caught my breath. The ram was going to charge.

I looked back at Todd. He was in a dead run for the ram. "Benadryl!" he shouted as he vaulted the fence.

The artist, seeing Todd running at him, waved and shook his head. "Oh, I don't mind. He's just being friendly." He glanced back at the ram, who was nibbling his pants. "Aggressively friendly. I don't mind."

I watched Todd smile and nod, then lasso the ram with rope and tackle him to the ground. The ram bucked and twisted. I could tell Todd had had enough. He dragged the ram, kicking and snorting, across the field.

I didn't wait to see the rest. I jumped in the car and headed for the store. I was pretty sure I was done with honeybees for a while. I had a feeling Todd was, too.

Most of our Saturday mornings look something like that.

◆◆◆◆

The good life is also a lot of work. We keep thinking that one day we'll get things fixed and organized so it won't be as much work. By now, all the fences need replacing. Every single one. That will take months and thousands of dollars.

The good life is so much work that we don't do much recreating. By the time Sunday rolls around and we've put in our day jobs and the twenty hours a week weeding, mowing, fencing, fixing, and watering, hiking twelve miles for an hour of fishing doesn't sound that fun.

But I'll tell you what. I love our life. I absolutely love it. Every evening when the sun slips down in the sky and the shadows lengthen towards the river, I feel this great love. I love the way the grass is green near the river and the owls that startle in the forest. I love hearing the kingfisher chatter as he flies overhead and the snaky little mink among the river rocks.

I even love the cows with their huge dark eyes and wet black noses. I love the munching sound they make when I throw them hay. And the sheep with their tiny hooves and nervous baaing. I love the first blueberries and the first tomatoes. I love making a dinner where every ingredient comes from this ten acres. The truth is, I have had the *best* life here in the Methow.

I used to think I should move. Kids who grow up here are supposed to leave. Most of them aren't supposed to come back. I left—for bits of time. As an anthropologist and student, I've lived and traveled in more than forty countries around the world. And I'm grateful for this, too. I've been incredibly fortunate. But mostly, I'm grateful that I've spent my life in wild places. I've listened to the wind in the trees and felt the sun on my face almost every day of my life.

I know people are moving here. People are moving to all the rural places in the world. I know we have to share.

You will love it here. There is so much to enjoy about the good life.

I'd like to say that everything that matters here is free, but that's not true. Our farm would sell today for more than we could ever afford in our lifetime. I find it sad that simple things like growing your own tomatoes and watching the sun set over a field cost money. They shouldn't, but they do. I can't fix a society that privileges the privileged again and again. But I can tell you this way of life is worth every penny.

Listen for the silences. They're never silent. Turn off your phones and disconnect. The world is a magical place. And this truly *is* the good life.

Postscript

I started writing this book during August of 2020, the first summer of the Covid-19 pandemic.

At the time, I felt trapped. The trailheads were crowded, the swimming holes overrun with people. RVs dotted the hillsides—and everywhere the Methow felt like it was bursting at the seams. The girls and I tried to maintain our normal summer activities, but each foray out on a trail, bike ride, or swim felt like a siege. Dogs, kids, motorcycles, tourists. We'd hurry back home, grateful for the peace and quiet of our little farm.

During that month, we decided to spend the school year in Hawai'i. We packed up a few clothes, rented our house to some friends, and left for eight months. When we returned, it felt like a different country.

This had partly to do with me. Due to a health emergency, I spent seven weeks in various hospitals on the way home, where I literally fought for my life.

When I emerged in June of 2021, I was different. Nothing felt the same. I spent the first few weeks bemused. I had little to say. I was also completing the TwispWorks Comprehensive Economic Study, which had taken me two years of surveys, research, and writing. Together, these two experiences had a profound impact upon me and my family.

Since then, we have spent more time in Hawai'i than the Methow. You might say that we gave up on the good life.

But I don't see it like that.

Having spent so much of my life in the Methow Valley, trying to carve out a life, an identity, and a career, I realized that it might be time to let go.

Elsewhere, I've written about place-attachment. I still feel like you can love a place like you love a person, and I am still in love with the Methow Valley. I always will be. But the structures here have changed.

As I've written these chapters, the changes have become more solidified. The prices of homes have risen. There are more remote workers and more people moving to the valley. I don't know if my children will be able to come back to the place they still call home.

I have mixed feelings about the Methow today.

On one hand, I have come to know and love many of the remote workers and new retirees. Because of my job at TwispWorks, they have become my reference group. We've had dinners together and Zoom calls and visits in Hawai'i. I now consider these people to be my closest friends.

On the other hand, I know that I don't fit in their world. My husband and I are probably one of the last categorically *middle-class* households in the Methow Valley, and it's not enough.

There is also something about the culture of the new Methow that isn't me. I don't want the quality of my house to define me, any more than I want having been a housecleaner or barista to define who I am as a person.

I want my life to be about what I do with it, and I have a lot more to do.

To everyone who potentially reads this book—this is for you. Consider this my love letter to the Methow Valley. You will always be in my heart.

Julie Tate-Libby
May 1, 2025

Acknowledgements

This book would not have been possible without the help, encouragement and patience of many people. Many thanks to Don Linnertz, who offered suggestions and thoughtful critique. Thank you to Karen West for her encouragement, edits, and belief in the book. And to my publisher, Greg Wright, who eventually found this book and brought it to life, to my sister, Jen, who insisted I continue writing these essays, and to all the dear friends in Study Group who mentored me years ago—Diana, Bill, Peter, Jennifer, Karl, Leahe, Jerry, Richard, David, and especially James. Thank you, James, for helping me find my voice. Thank you to Mom and Dad, who instilled my early love for the mountains and wild places, and to Todd—for your love, patience, and encouragement over the years.

This book is for my daughters, Annika and Mia. *May you always find your way home.*

JULIE TATE-LIBBY is an anthropologist and writer from the Pacific Northwest. Her first book, *The Good Way: A Himalayan Journey* (Koehler Books, 2019) was a finalist for the 2020 Washington State Book Awards. Her work on amenity migration, the power of place, and sacred mountains has appeared in many academic publications, and her creative work has been featured in the *Cirque Journal* and on the Washington State Poet Laureate's website. Julie is also an avid teacher, gardener, and culinary enthusiast who splits her time between Washington State and Hawai'i.

www.ingramcontent.com/pod-product-compliance
Lightning Source LLC
Chambersburg PA
CBHW020743100426
42735CB00037B/326